Professional Upholstering

All the Trade Secrets

Professional Upholstering

All the Trade Secrets

Frank T. Destro, Jr.

Printed in the United States of America

ISBN: 978-0-9828883-0-8

Contents

Acknowledgement

I would like to offer a very special thank you to my wife and family for all of their help, inspiration, support, understanding and patience. I would also like to say thank you to the many skilled craftsmen who have shared their talents, skills and knowledge with me. To everyone that helped guide me through my career, and to all of my students, for giving me the opportunity to discover my love and passion for teaching, I thank you.

Introduction

Over 30 years ago, Frank T. Destro, Jr. was taught the fine art of custom upholstering from several craftsmen, as well as through his many trials and errors. With his knowledge and skills, you can restore your worn-out furniture back to the beautiful elegance it once had.

You will learn *All The Trade Secrets*, along with: basic tips, terminology, how to use upholstering tools, supplies, how to measure, match, and cut fabric, installation of webbing, and spring tying, as well as cushion, welt cord, and zipper making. You will also learn how to cut, sew, and upholster two styles of dining room seats, make a zippered pillow, a fully upholstered wing chair, and a foot stool. Every step of the way is clearly explained and photographed to make your upholstering projects as simple as possible.

There are a vast number of *Tips!* you should be aware of before starting your projects. To take full advantage of these tips, I recommend reading this book in its entirety, before starting your project.

In today's society everyone is looking for new ways to recycle. Reupholstering is an excellent way to recycle and keep our precious earth a little greener for years to come.

Disclaimer

Safety should always be your first consideration when upholstering. Power tools, hand tools, and many of the supplies used in the upholstering industry are inherently dangerous if not used properly. Always wear eye protection and follow the manufacturers' recommendations for safety when working with hand tools, power tools and chemicals.

The author and publisher of this book do not accept responsibility of any type, kind, or nature for any consequences arising from the application of any information, advice, or instruction given in this publication. Due to differing conditions, materials, and skill levels, the author, publisher, and manufacturers disclaim any liability for unsatisfactory results or injury due to improper use of tools, materials, or information in this publication.

Student's Projects

The following photos feature a few samples of projects completed by Frank's students. They all utilize the techniques discussed in this book.

Before You Start

Before you start your project you need to ask yourself a few questions. Is this a quality piece of furniture I wish to re-upholster? Is it a family heirloom? Do I like the style? How much time will this take me to complete? Is it worth my time, energy, and money?

Please read through each section of this book before starting your project. You will discover many *Tips!* and *All The Trade Secrets* to guide you through the process of selecting and purchasing tools, supplies, and fabric. This will save you valuable time and money. As an added benefit, a *Glossary of Terminology* is available at the back of the book with easy-to-understand descriptions for industry-specific terminology.

I recommend you start out with smaller projects, such as; dining room seats or pillows. This will help you learn as you go and make the larger projects seem effortless.

Once you decide to proceed with your project, find a suitable work area. This space should be large enough to accommodate your project, tools and supplies. Your cutting table can be set up here or in any other convenient location where you wish to cut your fabric. I recommend using a large cutting table. This will make measuring, marking, and cutting the fabric much easier. *Tip!* A simple and easy way to make a large cutting table is to place two (2) 8-foot long folding tables together. A sheet of *Masonite*, or any other smooth hard surface can be placed over the tabletops. This smooth hard surface will make marking and cutting the fabric much easier. *Tip!* If the tables are too low for your comfort, place a block of wood under each leg to raise the tables to the desired height. This will help eliminate strain on your back when measuring, marking, and cutting the fabric. If you are limited on space, your cutting table can easily be taken apart and stored in a matter of minutes.

Chapter 1 | Basic Tips and Trade Secrets

Figure 1-1

Figure 1-2

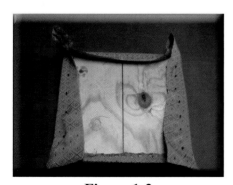

Figure 1-3

These tips and trade secrets apply to all forms of upholstering and are used daily in the making of pillows, cushions, dining room chair seats, cornice boards, headboards, chairs, and sofas.

Take pictures of your project before starting. This will enable you to refer back to them as needed.

The steps most commonly used in order to apply new fabric to upholstered chairs are as follows; deck, inside arms, inside wings, inside back, outside wings, outside arms, outside back, base welt trim, and cambric. If a skirt is to be added, apply the skirt and then cambric. The cushions should always be constructed last.

When removing the old fabric, start in the reverse order as above. Mark each piece of fabric that is removed. You can refer back to these pieces if needed.

Mark centers on all fabric pieces and on the frame (Figure 1-1). It is imperative to mark centers because all stripes and patterns will be centered on these center marks. If the centerlines are not properly marked, the stripes and patterns will be offset and not match. All fabric pieces should be measured from the center of the stripe or pattern outwards.

Loose tack all fabric before stapling (Figure 1-2). Loose tacking is a method of temporarily holding fabric in place before stapling. Place a tack on the small magnetic end of the tack hammer and nail the tack just enough to hold the fabric in place. The tack can easily be removed later. You may have to re-stretch and loose tack several times to smooth the padding or until the fabric is taut. Next, work from the centers outwards, removing the loose tacks as you replace with staples.

Always tack or staple opposite sides, such as back to front and top to bottom. This keeps an even stretch on the fabric and also keeps stripes and patterns very straight.

Side-to-side tacking or stapling is performed after the front to back or the top to bottom tacking or stapling is completed (Figure 1-3).

1

Corners are commonly upholstered last.

Use soft style chalk to mark on fabrics. The soft chalk is easily dusted off when needed.

Tip! To achieve a crisp line with your chalk, simply cut and angle it at the top with scissors.

Tip! Tailor's style chalk is very thin and waxy. It can be extremely difficult to remove. Use caution when marking with tailor's chalk. Tailor's chalk is commonly used for permanent marking.

When cutting your fabric, remember to always mark the backside with a large X. Label each piece, for example; inside arm, outside wing, and always mark top and bottom of each piece for easy identification.

When working with vinyl or lightly colored fabrics, chalk lines can be hard to see. Use a pencil to lightly mark on the backside of the fabric. *Tip!* Never use a marker or an ink pen to mark fabric. They will bleed through to the face of the fabric. This could be a costly mistake.

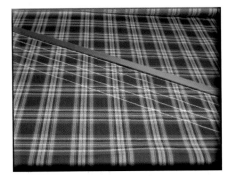

Figure 1-4

Tip! Keep your work area neat and organized. Once you have cut all the fabric pieces, place them in neat piles. Place all of the insides with insides, outsides with outsides, etc.

Tip! It's important to keep your work area clean of all debris. Always clean as you go. Loose tacks, staples, and tools on your work area can cause damage to exposed wood arms, legs and fabric.

When cutting your fabric, the welt cords are commonly cut last and on the bias (Figure 1-4). The bias means cut on a diagonal. Welt cords are each cut 1-1/2″ wide. You can cut a piece of wood 1 1/2″ wide and 60″ to 72″ long. This will be your welt stick and will be used to mark out all of the pieces of welt cord. Place the welt stick on a bias and strike a line on each side of the stick. Share one of the existing lines and strike another line. Continue doing this until all the pieces of welt are cut. For best results, cut all of the welt cords at one time. This ensures the same bias and will make all of the cords look the same. By cutting the welt cords on a bias, the fabric will be easier to work with and will wear longer. When working with all napped fabric, welt cords must be cut on a bias. If the welt cords are cut straight across the fabric from selvage to selvage, the backing of the fabric will show when the welt cord is made. The fabric will also wear much quicker. *Tip!* Be sure not to flip-flop any of the pieces of welt cord after cutting. If the cords are reversed when sewn together, the color can change drastically from piece to piece.

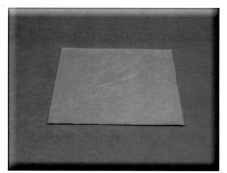

Figure 1-5

Figure 1-6

Figure 1-7

Figure 1-8

When working with a napped fabric such as velvet (Figure 1-5), always apply the nap smooth from top to bottom, and smooth from back to front. Run your hand across the fabric from top to bottom, and then from bottom to top. You will feel the fabric ruffle in one direction and be smooth in the other direction. If the fabric is not applied in the same direction, the color will change. Try cutting a small piece of napped fabric such as velvet. Place it upside down and next to the area where it was cut from. Notice the difference in the color of the fabric.

When purchasing fabric, have the clerk roll the fabric on a cardboard tube. You do not want to have to remove wrinkles before starting your project. Ask the clerk to also roll the fabric face in and the pattern backwards (Figure 1-6). When you are ready to cut the fabric, you will simply start unrolling the fabric and the pattern will be facing you. You will not have to reach over the rolled area of the fabric. This also helps to keep the fabric clean. If the store clerk gives you a hard time about rolling the fabric in this fashion, tell them I told you to ask them to do this. Proceed to tell them about my book and all the great tips you learned.

When stripping off the old fabric from your chair, remove the cambric, base welt, skirt, outside back, outside arms, and outside wing fabric (Figure 1-7). Mark these pieces and store them for later reference, if needed. Remove the remaining staples or tacks from the fabric on the inside areas of the chair. Leave the old fabric on the inside areas of the chair intact and remaining on the chair until you are ready to install the new fabric to that area. This will prevent the old fillings from shifting. Loose tack this remaining fabric to hold it in place. When loose tacking the fabric on the bottom of the inside back and inside arms, tack the fabric on the upper part of the stretcher rails. This will allow the new deck fabric to pass through later.

When stapling the fillings or fabric, always keep the staples parallel to the edge of the wood frame (Figure 1-8). If the staples are placed perpendicular to the wood frame only a small amount of fabric will be held in place. A pull mark will most likely appear in this area. When working with lighter weight or finer fabrics, remember to place the staples closer together to avoid pull marks. Do not place the staples too close to the edge of the frame.

If you are getting annoyed and frustrated with a certain step, stop and take a break and come back to it later. Always remember, "If upholstering was easy, there would be a shop on every corner."

Chapter 2 | Yardage Chart

12 yds	10 yds	12 yds	12 yds	12 yds	14 yds	10 yds
12 yds	14 yds	14 yds	12 yds	6 yds	11 yds	7 yds
12 yds	10 yds	10 yds	12 yds	12 yds	5 yds	10 yds
8 yds	8 yds	7 yds	8 yds	5 yds	5 yds	2 yds
2 1/2 yds	3 yds	5 yds	6 yds	7 yds	6 1/2 yds	6 1/2 yds
6 1/2 yds	6 1/2 yds	6 1/2 yds	6 yds	6 yds	5 1/2 yds	5 yds
6 1/2 yds	5 yds	6 yds	7 yds	6 yds	6 yds	6 yds
5 1/2 yds	4 1/2 yds	3 1/2 yds	4 1/2 yds	4 yds	4 1/2 yds	5 yds
7 yds	6 yds	4 yds	6 yds	*Allow approximately 20% extra yardage for pattern matching.		

4

Chapter 3 | Conversion Chart - Inches to Metric

Measurements

Inches	Centimeters
1 in.	2.5 cm.
2 in.	5.1 cm.
3 in.	7.6 cm.
4 in.	10.1 cm.
6 in.	15.2 cm.
1 ft.	30.5 cm.
1 yd.	91.5 cm.

Chapter 4 | Conversion Chart - Fractions to Decimals

Fraction	Decimal	Fraction	Decimal
1/64	.015625	33/64	.515625
1/32	.03125	17/32	.53125
3/64	.046875	35/64	.546875
1/16	.0625	9/16	.5625
5/64	.078125	37/64	.578125
3/32	.09375	19/32	.59375
7/64	.109375	39/64	.609375
1/8	.125	5/8	.625
9/64	.140625	41/64	.640625
5/32	.15625	21/32	.65625
11/64	.171875	43/64	.703125
3/16	.1875	11/16	.6875
13/64	.203125	45/64	.703125
7/32	.21875	23/32	.71875
15/64	.234375	47/64	.734375
1/4	.25	3/4	.75
17/64	.265625	49/64	.765625
9/32	.28125	25/32	.78125
19/64	.28125	51/64	.796875
5/16	.3125	13/16	.8125
21/64	.328125	53/64	.828125
11/32	.34375	27/32	.84375
23/64	.359375	55/64	.859375
3/8	.375	7/8	.875
25/64	.390625	57/64	.890625
13/32	.40625	29/32	.90625
27/64	.421875	59/64	.921875
7/16	.4375	15/16	.9375
29/64	.453125	61/64	.953125
15/32	.46875	31/32	.96875
31/64	.484375	63/64	.984375
1/2	.50	1	1.00

Chapter 5 | Wing Chair Frame Structure

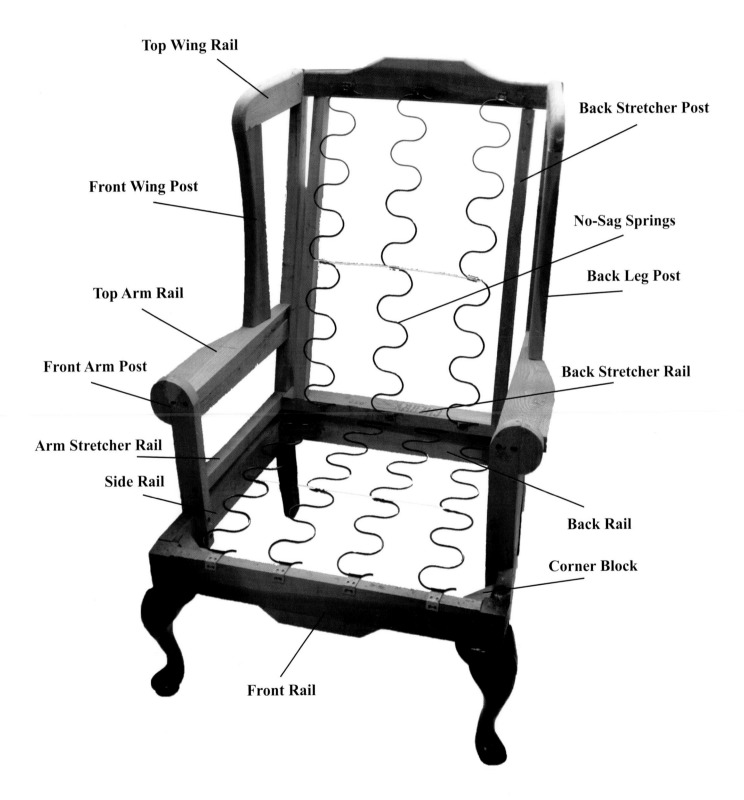

Top Wing Rail

Back Stretcher Post

Front Wing Post

No-Sag Springs

Top Arm Rail

Back Leg Post

Front Arm Post

Back Stretcher Rail

Arm Stretcher Rail

Side Rail

Back Rail

Corner Block

Front Rail

Chapter 6 | Frame Repair

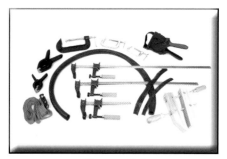

Figure 6-1

Figure 6-2

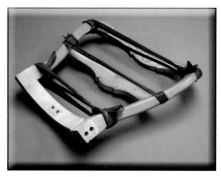

Figure 6-3

Many types of clamps can be used when regluing and repairing furniture frames. Bar clamps, strap clamps, and C-clamps are commonly used. Sometimes a combination of clamps will be needed at the same time (Figure 6-1). ***Tip!*** When working with oddly shaped frames such as antiques, it can be difficult to use these standard style clamps. An old bicycle inner tube can be the best device to use when a clamp will not work properly. Cut out the air valve section of the inner tube and discard. Cut the inner tube lengthwise in half, quarters, or thirds, depending on the strength desired and the application. When working with small cracks, curved shaped backs, oddly shaped arms or decorative wood surfaces, I like to use an inner tube (Figure 6-2). The inner tube will not damage carved or decorative wood finishes. To use the inner tube instead of a clamp when gluing a small crack, simply pull the inner tube very tight around the wood and knot the ends together. When gluing oddly shaped areas together, knot one end of the inner tube around the section to be glued and pull the inner tube until you are satisfied with the tightness. Wrap the inner tube around the other area to be glued and knot the end of the inner tube to complete. Let the glue dry completely before removing any type of clamp. Always follow the manufacturers' directions for use when using any adhesive (Figure 6-3).

Bar clamps are normally used to hold long areas of the frame together. The front to back, side to side, and the upright rails are commonly held in place with bar clamps (Figure 6-4). Strap clamps can be used with square frames, but are most commonly used to hold rounded frames together (Figures 6-5 through 6-8). C-clamps are normally used to hold two or more pieces of wood together, or to hold the splits and cracks in the frame together when glued (Figures 6-9 & 10).

Wood screws can be added to the repaired area but should not be needed. If wood screws must be used, countersink the screw heads to prevent damage to the padding or fabric, and always pre-drill the screw holes to help prevent the wood from cracking or splitting. Do not use nails when making frame repairs. Nails tend to back their way out of the frame and do not hold as well as screws.

Figure 6-4

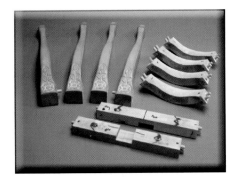

Figure 6-5

Figure 6-6

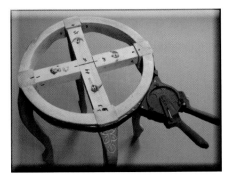

Figure 6-7

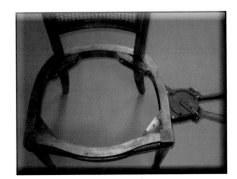

Figure 6-8

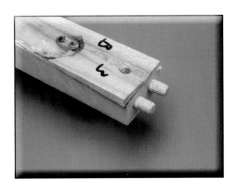

Figure 6-9

Figure 6-10

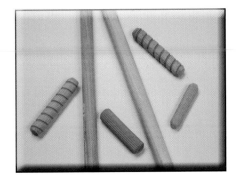

Figure 6-11

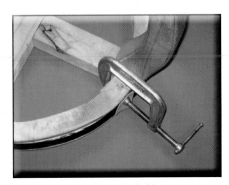

Figure 6-12

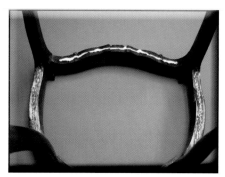

Figure 6-13

Figure 6-14

When wood dowel pins need to be replaced because they are broken, cut the existing dowel pins flush with the frame and drill out the remaining broken dowel pin. Drill the correct diameter hole and replace the broken dowel pin with the same diameter dowel pin (Figure 6-11). Add wood glue to the dowel pin and use clamps to make a tight joint when gluing the frame back together. Most dowel pins are made with grooves to permit the glue to spread throughout the joint.

Always use extreme caution when gluing or making repairs on frames with exposed wood finishes. To prevent damaging the exposed wood surfaces, pieces of rubber webbing, soft wood, or other padded materials should be used between the end of the clamp and the exposed wood surface before gluing. Some clamps are sold with rubber caps already attached (Figure 6-12).

If the rails are slightly cracked or have several holes from previous tacking, wood glue should be applied across the rails and pushed down into the holes with your finger. Be careful not to get splinters from the wooden rails. This will help strengthen the rails. Let the glue dry before applying the webbing (Figure 6-13).

Whether you are gluing an entire chair frame or making small repairs to the frame, always use high quality wood glue. I prefer to use *Titebond* brand wood glues. When working on marine projects, I prefer to use *Titebond II* because it is water resistant. These high-quality wood glues are non-toxic and clean up easily with water. *Titebond* wood glue products are manufactured by *Franklin International* (Figure 6-14).

Chapter 7 | Installing Webbing

Figure 7-1

Figure 7-2

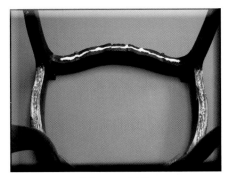

Figure 7-3

Webbing is used to create a base or foundation to support coil springs or padding. If you are using coil springs in the seat area, the webbing should be installed on the bottom of the chair rails. If you are using padding such as foam instead of coil springs, the webbing will be installed on the top of the rails.

To create a very strong foundation, it is important to tack or staple the webbing strips as close together as possible. Use as many strips of webbing that will fit into the frame. *Tip!* Cut two pieces of webbing approximately 2″ in length. Use these pieces as a gauge to layout the webbing pattern. By placing the webbing pieces next to each other and moving them along the rail you can determine how many pieces of webbing will be needed, and where to place them. After you have an idea of where the webbing will be placed, start working from the back of the chair to the front of the chair (Figure 7-1). **Do not precut the strips of webbing.** *Tip!* Examine the chair's frame rails where the webbing will be tacked or stapled. If the rails are slightly cracked or have several holes from previous tacking (Figure 7-2), wood glue should be applied across the rails and pushed down into the holes with your finger (Figure 7-3). Be careful not to get splinters from the wooden rails. This will help strengthen the rails. Let the glue dry before applying the webbing.

Working from the back to the front, fold over approximately 3/4″ to 1″ of webbing at the end of the strip and attach the folded end to the frame with four #12 or #14 upholstering tacks. *Tip!* When tacking webbing into place, remember to keep the folded edge of the webbing a slight distance from the outside edges of the frame. Welt cord or some other type of trim may be applied later to the bottom edge of the chair frame. Keep this outer edge of the frame as smooth as possible. Always stagger the tacks when tacking the webbing into place. If the webbing tacks are tacked straight across the webbing they are more likely to split the wood (Figure 7-4). The second step is to stretch the webbing to the front rail. Pull the webbing to the front and place the rubber end of the webbing stretcher up to the front of the wood rail. Move the spiked end of the webbing stretcher approximately 2″ to 3″ above level. Hook the webbing through the teeth of the webbing stretcher (Figure 7-5). *Tip!* The teeth are extremely sharp. Use caution! Push downwards with one hand until the webbing is very tight

Figure 7-4

Figure 7-5

Figure 7-6

Figure 7-7

(Figure 7-6). At this time, tack three or four webbing tacks across the strip of webbing. Release the webbing stretcher and cut the webbing approximately 1″ longer in length from where you tacked the webbing. Fold webbing over and tack 3–4 more tacks across the webbing, staggering the tacks and keeping the fold away from the very edge of the frame. Folding the end of the webbing and tacking it twice makes it much stronger and prevents it from fraying. *Tip!* If you are applying webbing to an antique or an older piece of furniture with frail wooden rails, the webbing tacks can be replaced with 9/16" staples. Using the narrow staples instead of large webbing tacks, and adding wood glue to the minor cracks and old tack holes, helps to prevent the older wooden rails from splitting.

After the front to back pieces of webbing have been installed, install the side-to-side pieces of webbing. These pieces will be applied the same way the front to back pieces were applied, with the exception of being interwoven (Figure 7-7). Start the first side-to-side piece of webbing in the front of the frame. The next side-to-side piece of webbing should be started very close to the first piece. The second piece will be applied opposite the first. If you started the first piece under the webbing running from front to back, the second piece will be started over the webbing running from front to back. This basket weaving technique makes the foundation very strong. Now you are ready to install the coil springs (Figure 7-8).

Steel webbing may be added to the webbing at this time to provide additional support to the jute or polypropylene webbing. It should be stretched over the webbing in the center of each coil spring (Figure 7-9). It is then interwoven and secured to the frame with stronghold or ring shank nails. A specialty tool called a metal webbing stretcher should be used to apply this type of webbing (Figure 7-10).

If your chair seat is designed not to have springs or you would like to replace the springs with foam, the webbing will most likely be installed the same way but on the top of the rails. The springs can be replaced with padding such as foam and cotton or polyester batting. Jute webbing does not have any spring or give to it. It is a very solid foundation. *Tip!* If your chair is designed to have webbing on the top of the rails, elastic webbing is a better choice than jute webbing. The elastic webbing provides a spring like action when sat upon (Figure 7-11). The elastic webbing is installed just like the jute webbing but with the help of a rubber & elastic webbing stretcher tool or it can be installed by pulling the elastic tightly by hand.

Some furniture such as Danish Modern style will use 2″ rubber webbing as a foundation. This type of webbing can be installed with sta-

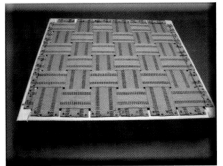

Figure 7-8

ples, tacks, or with clips installed on each end of the precut lengths (Figure 7-12). These clips are called rubber webbing clips and can be applied to the ends of the webbing with the use of a vise. The clips are placed into slots that are cut into the frame of the furniture. The seat cushions are placed directly on top of the rubber webbing.

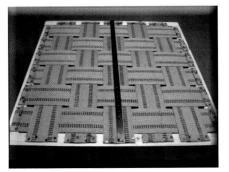

Figure 7-9

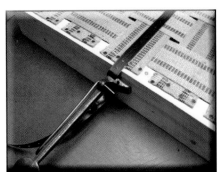

Figure 7-10

Figure 7-11

Figure 7-12

Chapter 8 | Spring Tying

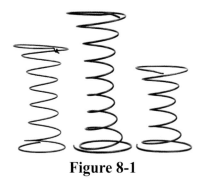

Figure 8-1

Figure 8-2

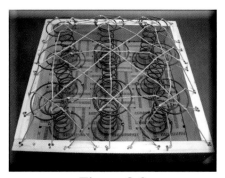

Figure 8-3

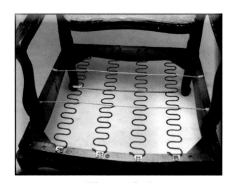

Figure 8-4

Springs are used in furniture as a foundation to provide support and comfort. These springs will be either coil springs (Figure 8-1), or No Sag springs (Figure 8-2). No Sag springs are also called Zig Zag or sinuous springs. Both of these types of springs are made of steel and come in different weights and gauges. The thinner or lighter gauges are used in the backs and the thicker or heavier gauges are used in the seats. Most mass-produced furniture use No-Sag springs. This is because the furniture manufacturers save time and money using this process. It is less expensive to cut the No Sag springs to size and connect them to the furniture frames with spring clips rather than paying an upholsterer the additional time it takes to apply webbing and then hand tie the coil springs. Hand tying coil springs is very time consuming and will add additional costs to most furniture. The best possible spring system for seating is the 8 way, hand tied coil springs (Figure 8-3). This system offers the most support and comfort and will last for years to come.

Normally, the No Sag springs are tied together two or three times. These ties are made from one side of the frame to the other. Tying the springs makes them act as a unit, as opposed to individually. Some furniture manufacturers use a heavy gauge wire that is clipped to the springs instead of tying them (Figure 8-4). If you have a broken wire, simply replace it by removing the old clips and wire and then tie the springs together with spring twine. If you have a broken No-Sag spring it can be easily replaced. Make sure the length and gauge of the spring is the same as the old spring you are replacing. Replace the broken No Sag spring and continue by retying the springs and adding burlap over the springs.

When using coil springs, the first step is to secure the coils to the webbing. This is done professionally by using a tool called a Klintch-it. This tool secures the coil springs to the webbing with a small, very sharp metal clip (Figure 8-5). Three to four clips are used to fasten each coil spring to the webbing (Figure 8-6). For the do-it-yourselfer, a curved needle and button twine can be used to secure the springs to the webbing. *Tip!* Make sure the curved or tied end of the coil spring is upwards and the flat end of the coil spring is secured to the webbing. The curved end of the coils helps to prevent the knots from sliding off the open end of the coil spring. Place the coil springs over the webbing in neat rows. *Tip!* Use the stripes on the webbing as a guide to help position the

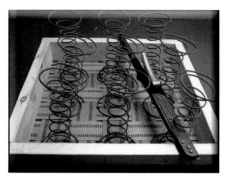

Figure 8-5

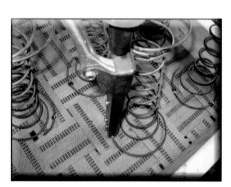

Figure 8-6

Figure 8-7

Figure 8-8

Figure 8-9

Figure 8-10

Figure 8-11

Figure 8-12

Figure 8-13

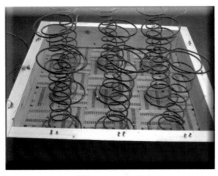

Figure 8-14

Figure 8-15

springs. *Tip!* All open ends of the coil springs should be positioned so that they are facing inwards. You will not want the open end of the coils on any of the outside edges. The open end of the spring is the weakest point of the spring. You want the outside edges of the springs to be very strong and supportive (Figure 8-7). Using a curved needle and button twine, sew the twine tightly through the webbing and around the base of the coil spring. Do this approximately four times and in three to four areas on the bottom of each spring. Make a secure knot to finish each tie. The second method will be slightly different. Form a knot holding one coil spring to the webbing. With one long continuous twine, knot three areas on the bottom of each coil spring. Continue this process until all of the coil springs are sewn to the webbing. Once the springs are secured to the webbing, it is time to start tying the springs (Figure 8-8).

Torsion springs can be added to the front corners of the coil springs to add strength to the corners (Figure 8-9). The top edge of the torsion spring is clipped to the top edge of the coil spring using an edge wire clip (Figure 8-10). The bottom end of the torsion spring is fastened to the frame using a No Sag spring clip (Figure 8-11).

When tying coil springs, determine if the springs are going to have a loose cushion on top of them or padding and the fabric. If the seat is going to have a loose cushion, the end result should be a very flat surface to accommodate the cushion (Figure 8-12). If the seat is padded, without a loose cushion, the springs will have a curved or crowned look to them when completed. This is called a tight seat (Figure 8-13).

Start tying the springs by loose tacking two #12 webbing tacks next to each other on the top of the rails and center them in line with each row of springs. Perform this step on all four sides. Cut spring twine for each row of springs, front to back and side to side. Measure the length of the frame and add 1/2 to 3/4 of the length to the measurement. This will allow for knotting and tacking to the frame (Figure 8-14). Start in the back and in the center row of springs. Make a loop at the end of the spring twine. Wrap it around one of the two tacks, pull it tight and hammer the tack into the frame (Figure 8-15). Next wrap the spring twine around the other tack and hammer it to the frame. Do this step to the remaining rows of springs in the back of the chair. Now hammer the twines into place on the left or the right side of the chair. *Tip!* I am right handed and would prefer to tie the springs from my left to my right. If you are right handed, repeat this step on the left facing side of the chair. If you are left handed, repeat this step on the right facing side of the chair. Now it is time to tie the springs. You will be working from the back to the front and just like all other steps in upholstering, starting in the center. When tying the springs from the back to the front

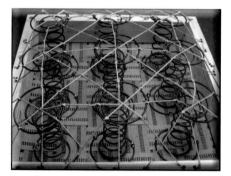

Figure 8-16

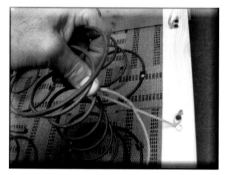

Figure 8-17

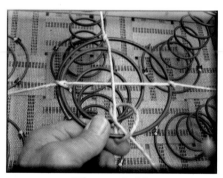

Figure 8-18

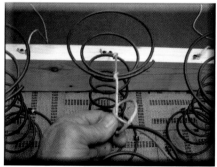

Figure 8-19

and from side to side, the first knot and last knot will be tied on the second or third coil down from the top. Only the diagonally tied knots will be tied on the top coil of all the outside edges. When the springs are tied lower on the outside edges it creates more of a spring action. If all of the knots were tied on the top coils, it would deaden the spring effect and create a motionless spring (Figure 8-16).

Start with the center spring in the back row. Coil springs are normally compressed approximately 2″ below their actual height when tied into position. Push down on the spring and place the twine **under** the second or third coil down. While still holding down the spring, loop the twine over the coil and pinch the two pieces of twine to the spring (Figure 8-17). Make sure the spring is tilting slightly backwards. I will explain why briefly: You do not want the spring to move now. Keep pinching the twine and spring together. Loop the end of the twine over the incoming twine and then pull the end of the twine through the opening to form a knot (Figure 8-18). Still holding the spring down and still pinching the twine to the spring, pull the twine very tight to cinch the knot to the spring. This will form a very strong knot. Yes, it would be nice to have three hands now. It will get easier as you continue. Now tie the next knot on the front of the back spring and on the very top coil. Pull the twine **under** the coil. Always start tying by placing the twine **under** the coil (Figure 8-19). With the twine under the coil, fold it over the top of the coil and pull the twine towards the back. When the twine is tight, pinch the twine and the coil together. Again, loop the end of the twine over the incoming twine and pull the end of the twine through the opening to form a knot. Pull the twine very tight to cinch the knot in place. Repeat this knot tying on the top coils until you get to the front coil on the front spring. This knot will be tied on the third coil down from the top. Remember when I said, have the coils slightly tilted backwards when you make the knots? Now you are going to pull the twine very firmly to the front. This will pull the springs forward and downwards, making them stand upright. If you need to, push down on the springs when you are pulling the twine forward. When the springs are upright, hold them in place by keeping the twine very tight and loop the spring twine around one of the two tacks on the front rail. With the twine pulled tightly, drive the tack into the frame. Loop the twine around the other tack and hammer the tack into the frame. If you have a chair with a loose cushion, you will need to perform another step or two. If you have a tight seat chair, without a loose cushion, you can now cut the twine.

If you are tying coil springs for a loose cushion style chair, perform the following steps to complete the front row of springs. Take the end of the twine and loop it over the top coil and pull downwards. You will see the front edge of the coil move downwards as you pull down on the

Figure 8-20

Figure 8-21

Figure 8-22

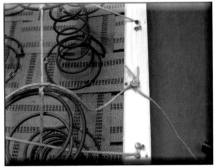

Figure 8-23

twine. You want to keep this coil as level as possible (Figure 8-20). Pull down on the twine until the front of the coil is level. When you see the coil is level, pinch the twine and coil together very tightly to hold in place. Now form a knot to hold the coil in this position. Pull the twine down and loop it around the second tack. Hammer the tack into the frame being careful to keep the front edge of the coil spring level (Figure 8-21). Continue the tying by pulling the twine from the tack over the front edge of the front coil again and forming another knot. Working towards the back now, continue forming knots on the top of the coils until you have knotted at least the front of the second spring again. If you still have twine remaining, you may continue tying or cut the twine at this point and complete the other rows of springs that are being tied from back to front (Figure 8-22). Make sure all of the springs are tied at the same height and pay particular attention to the front edge of the front row of springs. *Tip!* If you should run short on the spring twine you can tie two pieces together and continue (Figure 8-23).

The side-to-side rows of springs will be tied just like the front to back rows with the exception of the extra tying performed on the front springs. Working from side to side, the first knot and the last knot will be tied on the second or third coil down. After the first spring is tied, all of the other knots will be on the top of the coils with the exception of the last knot. Repeat this step on all the side-to-side tying (Figure 8-24).

The diagonal twines will now be tied in place. Cut a piece of twine approximately 3 feet long to be used as a gauge. Starting in the back and working towards the front and in a diagonal line, place the twine over the top of the coil springs. Start in either back corner and pull the twine tightly to the opposite side front leg. Keep the twine in the center of each coil to produce a straight line. Use this line as a gauge for your loose tack placement. *Tip!* Try not to tack into a corner block support. Corner blocks tend to be weaker than the frame and can easily split causing even more work. Repeat this step on the opposite side. Loop the twine around the first tack and hammer it into the frame. Then repeat on the second tack and start tying the diagonal rows. The first knot will be on the **top** of the coil (Figure 8-25). All the knots from this point on will be tied on the **top** coils (Figure 8-26). If you have a loose cushion, the first knot should be tied to keep the coil as level as possible. If you have a tight seat styled seat, pull the first twine slightly tighter. This will cause the spring to bend and create a curved effect on the edges (Figure 8-27). You'll then knot the spring in the desired position. Whatever style you have, you will finish the first row of diagonal twines the same way as you started the row. Repeat these steps working from back to front until each spring has eight knots on it. This is where the term "eight way, hand tied coil springs" comes from

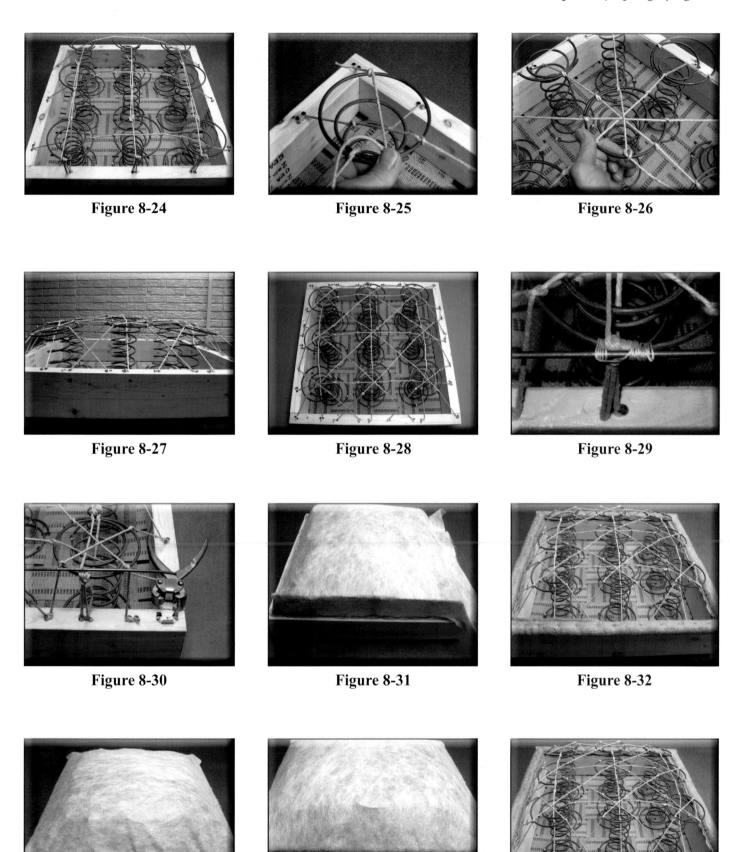

Figure 8-24

Figure 8-25

Figure 8-26

Figure 8-27

Figure 8-28

Figure 8-29

Figure 8-30

Figure 8-31

Figure 8-32

Figure 8-33

Figure 8-34

Figure 8-35

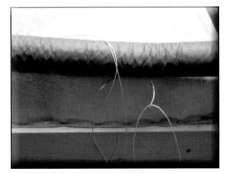

Figure 8-36

Figure 8-37

Figure 8-38

Figure 8-39

(Figure 8-28). *Tip!* You can cut the twine extra long when tying diagonal rows of springs. This will let you continue tying the springs without having to stop and cut twine for each individual row of springs.

If you have a loose cushion style chair the front row of springs may have had an edge wire attached to the front of them. You can now replace the wire. You can do this by either using edge wire clips, or by hand sewing it on with nylon button twine. If you hand sew the edge wire on, wrap the twine around the wire and the front of the coil spring several times to secure it in place (Figure 8-29). If you use the edge wire clips, a special type of pliers are made for this purpose called edge wire clip pliers (Figure 8-30). A pair of pliers or needle nose pliers can also be used to secure the edge wire clips.

At this point burlap is applied over the coil springs if you have a loose cushion style chair. Remember not to pull the burlap too tight. This can cause the edges of the coil springs to curve. When you staple the burlap to the chair rails make sure to staple and then cut approximately 3/4″ extra. Fold up this extra burlap and staple it again to prevent the burlap from fraying (Figure 8-31). Staple the burlap in the same location on the top of the rails you have tacked the spring twine into place. If you have a tight seat style chair, secure the edge roll to the frame and put the burlap over the edge roll (Figures 8-32, 33 & 34).

An edge roll will be applied at this time which is used to break the sharp edge of the springs or the sharp edge of the wooden frame. Edge roll comes in many diameters and styles. Edge rolls are designed to be stapled, tacked (Figure 8-35), hand sewn (Figure 8-36), or hog ringed into place (Figure 8-37). Hog rings are shaped like a C and have sharp ends to pierce through the edge roll. Professionals install hog rings with hog ring pliers. The hog ring pliers have a groove on each side of the jaws to hold the hog ring in place while pushing the hog ring through the edge roll and around the edge of a spring or edge wire (Figures 8-38 & 39).

If you push down on the front edge of the deck area and the result is a spring back effect, this type of edge is called a spring edge. It offers the most comfort but involves the most time and effort. If you push down on the front edge and nothing moves, this is called a hard edge. Some furniture is made this way because it is less expensive to add a wooden rail to the front of the furniture instead of taking the extra time involved to tie the springs differently.

If you have a loose cushion style chair, the deck area will be next. If you have a tight seat chair, start touching up the wood before you apply the padding over the springs.

Chapter 9 | Touching Up the Wood

Figure 9-1

Figure 9-2

Figure 9-3

Do not touch up the exposed wood surfaces on your project until just before the fabric is ready to be applied. You will most likely scratch the finished wood surfaces when removing the old fabric, applying webbing, tying the springs, or stapling new padding into place.

There are many methods used for touching up wood finishes. I have been using the following methods for many years, and with great success. If the wood surface has a few minor nicks or scratches, touch up the wood with *Old English Scratch Cover* (Figure 9-1), or *Minwax Wood Finish Stain Markers*. If the wood has minor holes or cracks, they can easily be filled with *Minwax Blend-Fil Pencil* (Figure 9-2). If the wood surfaces need a little more than a minor touchup, but does not need to be completely stripped and refinished, I like to use a combination of scratch cover or stain marker, spray lacquer, and then a clear protective finish to complete the process (Figure 9-3).

When you are ready to touch up the wood, apply rubber gloves to protect your fingers from being stained. To use *Old English Scratch Cover* simply apply a small amount of the scratch cover onto a clean cloth, wipe over the nick or scratch and wipe off the excess with a clean cloth (Figure 9-4). When I am working with a very small scratch or nick, I like to use a cotton swab to apply the scratch cover. *Old English Scratch Cover* is made for light and dark colored woods. To use *Minwax Wood Finish Stain Marker*, shake the marker well, remove the cap, and depress the tip gently a few times on paper or wood to start the stain flowing. Apply the stain to the wood. If needed, wipe any excess with a clean cloth (Figure 9-5).

If the wood needs more than a minor touch up, start by using a small scrubbing pad or a fine steel wool pad. Load up the pad with *Old English Scratch Cover* and rub it firmly onto the wood surface. Next, wipe off all of the excess scratch cover with a clean cloth until the surface is clean and the remnants of the scratch cover have been completely removed. The wood surface will now look like it has been refinished. Although the wood will look unbelievably better, spray staining the wood should be your next step to a complete touchup.

I like to use a spray lacquer made by *Cypress Point LLC*. *Cypress Point LLC* makes professional grade finishes and toners. These lacquer wood

Figure 9-4

Figure 9-5

Figure 9-6

finishes comes in many colors to match most wood finishes and they dry in minutes! (Figure 9-6) The lacquer wood finish is applied very similar to spray painting. After the finish has dried, apply a coat of *Cypress Point LLC* clear protective finish to complete the wood touch up process. The clear finishes come in several finishes. They are clear flat, satin clear flat, ultra flat clear, shellac, and flat oil finish. My personal favorite is satin clear flat.

When using any stain, lacquer, wood finish, or aerosol, always refer to the manufacturers' directions for use, and use only with adequate ventilation.

CYPRESS™ SPRAY LACQUERS
PROFESSIONAL GRADE FINISHES & TONERS

GUARANTEE
We guarantee all Cypress Point produts to cover as much surface, apply as easily, last as long and look as good as any similar products, regardless of name or price. We guarantee Cypress Point products will give satisfactory results whether applied by professional or amateur, if used according to instructions.

WOOD STAINS 100 SERIES
A combination of pigment, light resistant stains, seal and lacquer. Will cover any scratched or marred surface.

WOOD STAINS 200 SERIES
A combination of stain, sealer and lacquer. Used primarily on a new wood or where the grain should be visible.

ALSO AVAILABLE:

300 Clear Flat
301 Satin Clear Flat
302 Ultra Flat Clear
303 Gloss Clear

305 Flat Oil Finish
306 Sanding Seater
307 Lacquer Leveler
308 Semi-Gloss Clear

307 Lacquer Leveler - will blend in and level out overspray and orange peel areas.

101 True Mahogany	102 Rock Maple	103 True Walnut	104 Cordovan Mahogany	105 French Walnut
106 Shadow Walnut	108 Deep Walnut	109 Sandy Fruitwood	110 Brown Mahogany	112 Nutmeg
113 Light Fruitwood	114 American Walnut	115 Raw Umber	116 Burnt Umber	117 True Maple
118 Provincial Maple	119 Medium Walnut	120 Dark Oak	121 Red Mahogany	122 Extra Dark Walnut
201 Natural Walnut	202 Natural Mahogany	203 Natural Maple	205 Natural Oak	206 Van Dyke Brown
207 Golden Oak	401 Gloss Black	402 Ebony Black	403 Natural White	404 Antique White

NOTE: All colors shown have been reproduced as accurately as possible. Final results will vary, according to type and color of wood to be stained.
We suggest testing stains for color in an inconspicuous place before making the entire application.

Chapter 10 | Fabric Layout Diagrams

Fabric Shown "Railroaded"

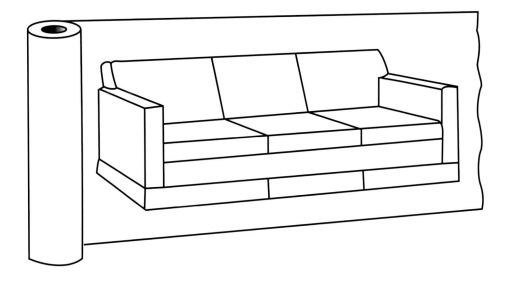

Fabric Shown "Up the Roll"

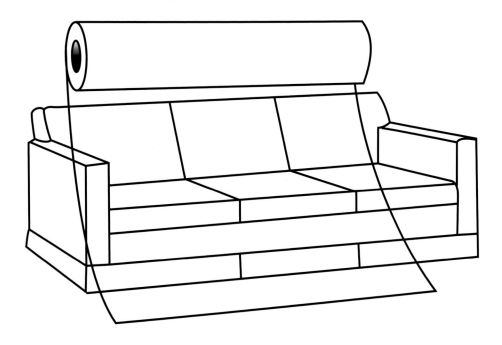

Chapter 11 | Measuring Fabric

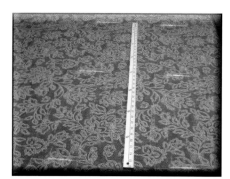

Figure 11-1

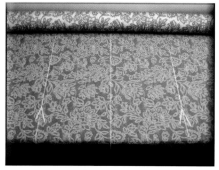

Figure 11-2

Figure 11-3

The following are basic tips to consider before you begin to measure.

Start measuring with the old fabric still remaining on the chair. Record the measurements of each piece needed. Remember to measure at the widest point of each piece. Make sure to add approximately 2″ to 3″ to each side to allow for pulling and stapling. When an item such as a cushion top is measured, add only 1/2″ to each side to allow for seams. This is because it will be sewn on the machine using 1/2″ seam allowances. *Tip!* **Do not cut the final size of the cushion tops yet.** Cut the cushion tops when the chair is completed. The measurements of your cushion can change if the new fabric was pulled tighter than the old fabric or if new padding was added to the old padding. If the old cushion measures 22″ from side to side, you would be safe to cut each cushion top 27″ from side to side. Most upholstery fabrics are 54″ wide. By cutting the fabric in half, you will be able to get two of the same 27″ wide fabric pieces from the width of the fabric. This will give you plenty of fabric to work with when the time comes to cut the cushion tops to fit the completed chair.

Most patterned fabrics have a repeat. A repeat is the distance between the repeating patterns (Figure 11-1). Most patterns are printed or woven into the fabric with the pattern running up and down the roll, and in most cases one side of the fabric will look identical to the other side (Figure 11-2). This is called up the roll. If the pattern or stripe is printed or woven from selvage to selvage, as opposed to up the roll, it is called railroaded (Figure 11-3). If the item you are recovering is wider than the standard 54″ width of fabric and if the fabric is not railroaded, you will have to sew widths of fabric together to achieve the desired width. You will also have to match the patterns. This can lead to extra time and extra fabric. If you are recovering an item that requires more than one 54″ width of fabric it may be wise to purchase a patterned fabric that is railroaded.

If your pattern repeat is 27″ and the piece you are measuring is only 5″, such as the boxing of the cushion, you will still need 27″ of fabric to match the pattern properly (Figure 11-4). You will have a loss of fabric between repeats. With this scrap fabric you can cut zipper tracks, boxing, and arm panels. To give you another example, let's say the repeat

Figure 11-4

Figure 11-5

Figure 11-6

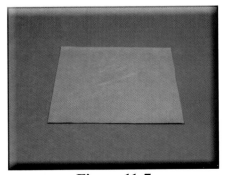

Figure 11-7

of your fabric is 9″ and the inside arms should be cut at 22″ from top to bottom, you will need 27″ of fabric to center and match the pattern properly. If the repeat is 9″, two repeats will be 18″, and three repeats will be 27″. You will need three full repeats when measuring out the fabric. You will need three full repeats at 9″ each, for a total of 27″ for your 22″ cut. Most of the time the fabric can be split down the center to get both inside arms, outside arms, and cushion tops out of the width of 54″ fabric (Figure 11-5). If the cushion is T-shaped, in most cases you will be unable to cut both cushion tops from the width of fabric.

Drop matched patterns do not match from side to side. Drop matched patterns are staggered. For example, looking down onto the fabric the left side will have a large flower and on the right side the same flower will appear several inches down the roll (Figure 11-6). In most cases, more fabric is used when working with a drop match pattern. Drop matched patterns are better suited for draperies rather than upholstery.

If you are working with a napped fabric such as velvet, it must be applied with the nap running smoothly from the top of the chair to the bottom of the chair. The nap should also run smoothly from the back of the chair to the front of the chair. To determine which way is smooth, run your hand up and down the face of the fabric. In one direction it should feel smooth and in the other direction it should feel ruffled. When marking and applying your napped fabric be sure the nap is running in the proper direction. Be certain to mark the back of each piece so you know which is the top and bottom. If the fabric is applied upside down the color will change drastically (Figure 11-7).

To save fabric, a draw strip can be sewn onto one or more edges of the fabric to add to the length and width. The draw strip can be a scrap of the same fabric, or any other fabric that is woven tightly to prevent ripping when pulled and stapled. Draw strips are commonly added to the bottoms of the inside arms, the width of the inside arms, the bottom of the inside back, and the width of the inside back (Figure 11-8). If you do add a draw strip, make sure the seam will not show. I personally try not to use draw strips unless I am forced to. I would rather use slightly more fabric than to go through the extra work of cutting and sewing draw strips.

Welting, welt cord, or piping, is the round decorative cord that is sewn or stapled between the seams or around the edges of the frame. Each fabric-covered strip of welt cord is cut on a bias and is 1-1/2″ in width. A bias means, cut on a diagonal. The welt cord is normally cut last (Figure 11-9). Measuring in inches, total the length of all the welt cords to be used. Divide this number by 54. This will tell you the total number of pieces of welt cord you will need to cut and sew together in one

Figure 11-8

Figure 11-9

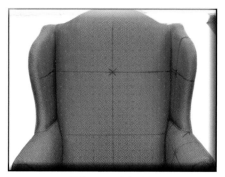

Figure 11-10

Figure 11-11

long piece. *Tip!* Most wing chairs require approximately 12 pieces of welt cord. *Tip!* Take the total length of the welt cord needed in inches, and divide that number by 36. This will tell you how many yards of the 5/32″ welt cord to purchase. When the pieces of fabric are cut for the welt cord, keep them all in the same direction that they were cut from the roll. Do not flip-flop the cut welt cord pieces. If the fabric is napped and the direction of the welt cords are changed from piece to piece when sewn together, the color of the fabric will change drastically.

Always purchase a little more fabric than needed. This will allow for mistakes and flaws in the fabric. Most fabric shops will give you an allowance if the fabric is flawed. *Tip!* If you measure your chair based on a plain fabric, add approximately 20% more fabric to allow for the pattern matching.

If you are using a striped or patterned fabric, mark reference lines on the old fabric before removing. These marks will help to center and match the stripes and patterns (Figures 11-10, 11 & 12). *Tip!* Using a yardstick and a marker, strike a line from the top of the inside wing to the deck area. Make sure this line is centered on the inside wing. Continue marking over the inside arm, and make sure the line is straight up and down (Figure 11-13). When laying out the new fabric you can use the old inside wing and inside arm fabric with the reference lines as a pattern or guide. Place these old pieces on top of the new fabric and line up the stripes or patterns on the new fabric (Figure 11-14). These reference lines will assure your stripes or patterns will match and line up with each other. If you are using the old pieces as a pattern, make sure to allow extra fabric for pulling, stapling, and sewing. *Tip!* If you have a pattern such as a floral bouquet, and would like to center the pattern on the inside back, measure from the top of the cushion to the top of the chair and not the top of the deck. This will give you a true center from the top of the cushion to the top of the chair. If you have a removable back cushion that sits on the seat cushion, be sure to deduct the thickness of the back cushion when centering a pattern on the seat cushion (Figures 11-15 & 16).

To continue the measuring process, list all of the pieces to be cut in the order that they will be applied to the chair. Then draw arrows to indicate the top to bottom measurements and the side-to-side measurements. Place these arrows next to each item to be cut. These arrows will help you keep your pattern, stripe, or napped fabric, running in the proper direction. Notice the X 2pc; this is to indicate 2 pieces of the same item will be needed. Once the measurements are taken, record them next to the appropriate names of each item. If you will be adding a skirt to your chair, add to your list, 4 skirt panels and 4 kickers.

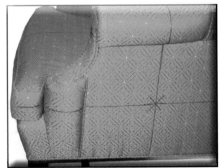

Figure 11-12

The zipper boxing fabric is cut 1-1/2″ larger than the **cut** size of the boxing. This allows for the flaps that will cover the zipper track.

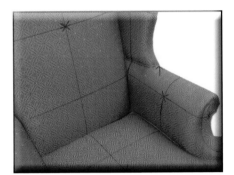

Figure 11-13

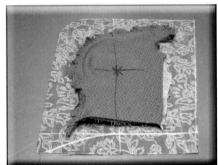

Figure 11-14

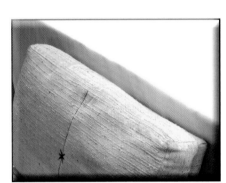

Figure 11-15

Figure 11-16

				↕	↔
		Deck		12″	50″
		Inside Arms	X 2pc.	27″	34″
		Inside Wings	X 2pc.	22″	16″
		Inside Back		42″	27″ + 8″ Draw Strips on Sides (if using them)
		Outside Wings	X 2pc.	25″	15″
		Outside Arms	X 2pc.	16″	27″
		Outside Back		38″	27″
		Cushion Tops	X 2pc.	24″	31″

				↕	↔
		Cushion Boxing	X 2pc.	4.5″	1 @ 54″ 1 @ 16″
		Zipper Boxing		6″	29″
		Arm Panels	X 2pc.	12″	6″
		Welt Cords	# of pieces needed (on the bias)	12pc.	

For your convenience, I've included the following blank worksheet for your use while you record your measurements.

				↕	↔
		Deck			
		Inside Arms	X 2pc.		
		Inside Wings	X 2pc.		
		Inside Back			
		Outside Wings	X 2pc.		
		Outside Arms	X 2pc.		
		Outside Back			
		Cushion Tops	X 2pc.		

				↕	↔
		Cushion Boxing	X 2pc.		
		Zipper Boxing			
		Arm Panels	X 2pc.		
		Welt Cords	# of pieces needed (on the bias)		

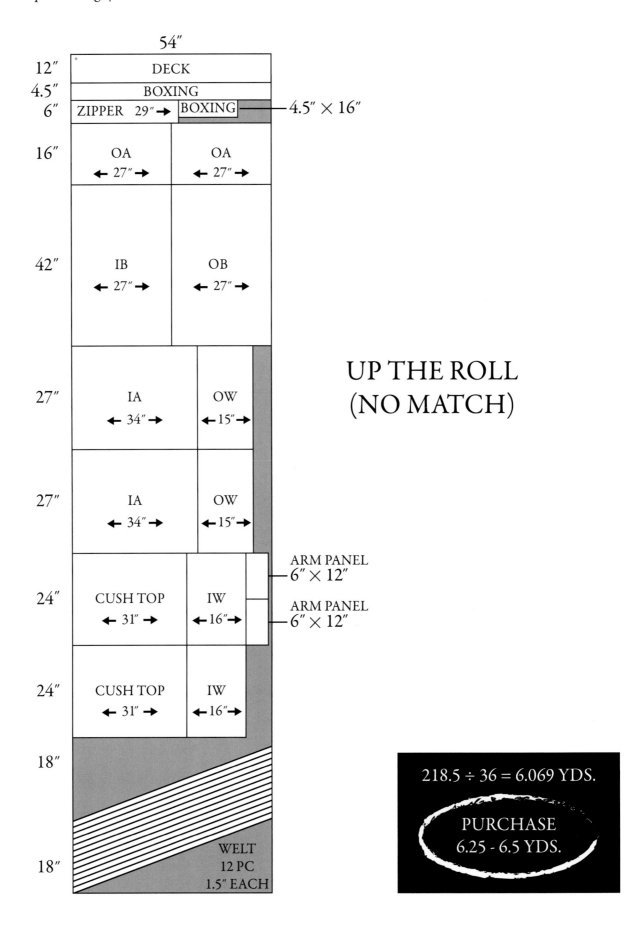

UP THE ROLL
(NO MATCH)

218.5 ÷ 36 = 6.069 YDS.

PURCHASE
6.25 - 6.5 YDS.

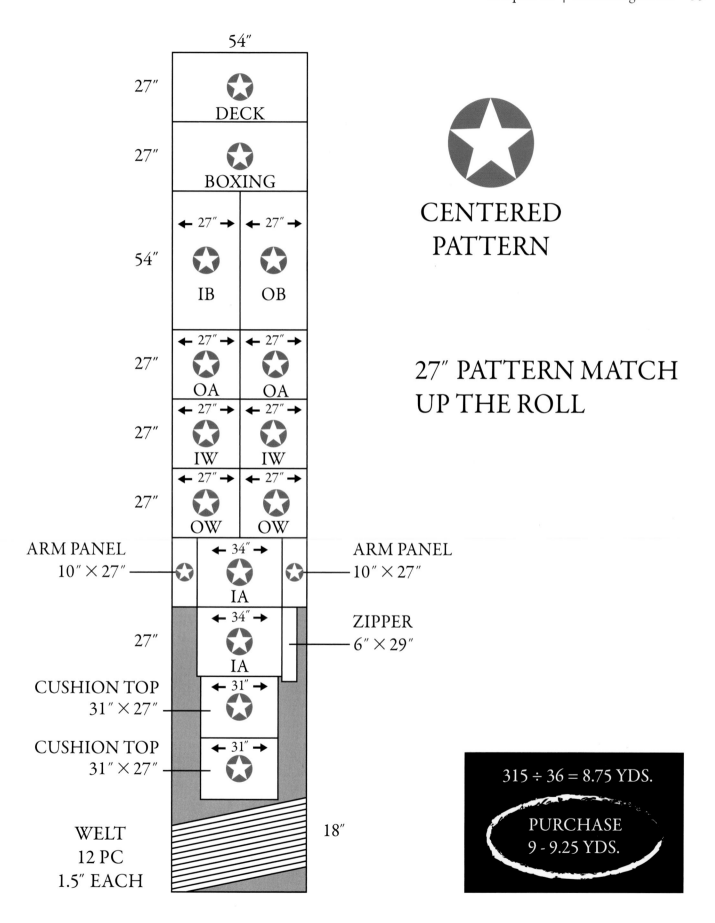

54"

27" DECK

27" BOXING

54" ← 27" → ← 27" →
IB OB

27" ← 27" → ← 27" →
OA OA

27" ← 27" → ← 27" →
IW IW

27" ← 27" → ← 27" →
OW OW

ARM PANEL
10" × 27" ← 34" → ARM PANEL
IA 10" × 27"

27" ← 34" → ZIPPER
IA 6" × 29"

CUSHION TOP
31" × 27" ← 31" →

CUSHION TOP
31" × 27" ← 31" →

WELT
12 PC
1.5" EACH 18"

CENTERED
PATTERN

27" PATTERN MATCH
UP THE ROLL

315 ÷ 36 = 8.75 YDS.

PURCHASE
9 - 9.25 YDS.

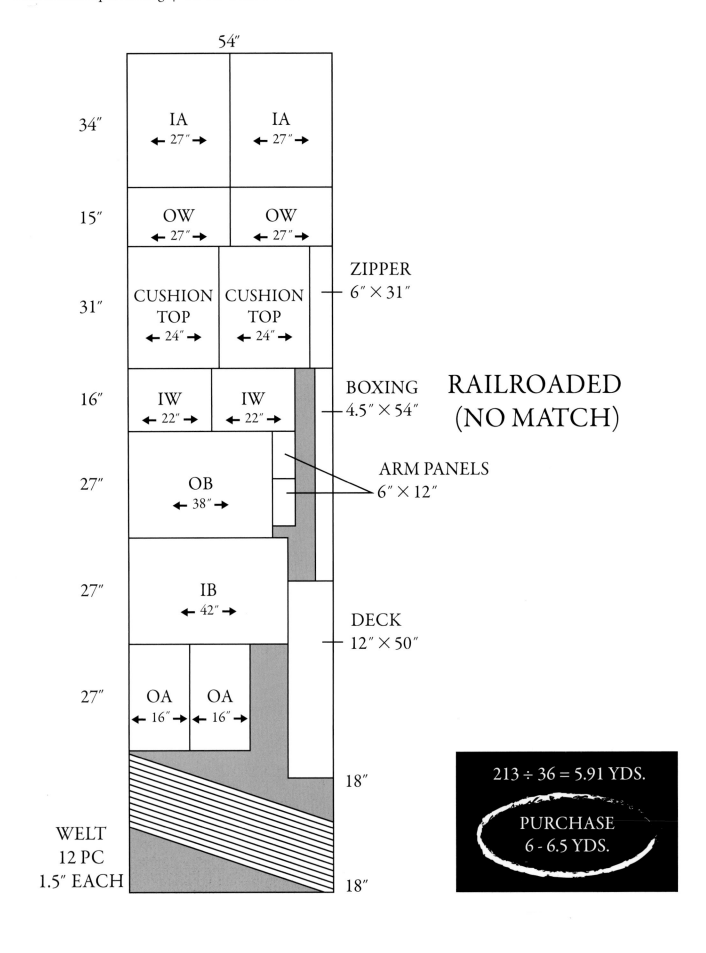

54"

34"

IA
← 27" →

IA
← 27" →

15"

OW
← 27" →

OW
← 27" →

31"

CUSHION
TOP
← 24" →

CUSHION
TOP
← 24" →

ZIPPER
6" × 31"

16"

IW
← 22" →

IW
← 22" →

BOXING
4.5" × 54"

RAILROADED
(NO MATCH)

27"

OB
← 38" →

ARM PANELS
6" × 12"

27"

IB
← 42" →

DECK
12" × 50"

27"

OA
← 16" →

OA
← 16" →

18"

WELT
12 PC
1.5" EACH

18"

213 ÷ 36 = 5.91 YDS.

PURCHASE
6 - 6.5 YDS.

Chapter 12 | Applying the Fabric

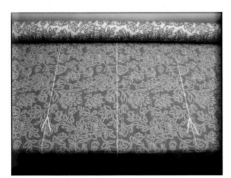

Figure 12-1

Figure 12-2

Figure 12-3

Section A: The Deck

Before you can cut your fabric for the deck, determine what pattern or stripe will be centered. If you are working with a large pattern such as a commonly used 27″ repeat, determine what pattern will be in the center of the seat and or back cushion. If a stripe is used, determine what color or pattern in the stripe will be centered. Most upholstery fabrics are 54″ wide and printed up the roll like wallpaper (Figure 12-1). It is common to split the 54″ width of fabric in half and have the same pattern on both sides (Figure 12-2). If your pattern is the same on both sides of the fabric, splitting this in half again will normally be your center. Most large patterns with a large repeat will have the identical large pattern on each side. If you drop down to the center of the roll, the same large pattern repeats itself in the center of the roll also. Two patterns across, drop down, one pattern in the center, drop down again, two patterns across, and so on (Figure 12-3). Most repeating fabrics will be laid out on the fabric in this fashion. With the fabric printed this way and splitting the fabric in half, both of the cushion tops, inside arms and the outside arms can sometimes be cut out of the full width of fabric (Figure 12-4).

In most cases T-shaped cushion tops and the deck fabric will have to be cut from the center of the fabric. This is because the width of the cushion tops and the deck fabric is greater than 27″ wide, which is one half of the width of the fabric. After the first cushion top is cut from the center of the fabric, drop down the roll of fabric and find the same pattern in the center of the fabric. This is where the next cushion top will be cut from (Figure 12-5).

Tip! If your chair has a back cushion and you need to find the center of the seat cushion, measure from the front of the back cushion to the front of the seat cushion (Figure 12-6). If you measure the length of the seat cushion and divide that measurement in half, your pattern would not be on center when your back cushion is placed on the seat cushion. (The centered pattern on your seat cushion will be placed forward the thickness of your back cushion.) This allows for the thickness of the back cushion when locating the centered pattern (Figure 12-7).

Figure 12-4

Figure 12-5

Figure 12-6

Figure 12-7

Figure 12-8

Figure 12-9

Figure 12-10

Figure 12-11

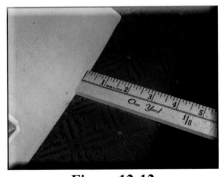

Figure 12-12

If a striped or plaid fabric is being used, the same principles will be applied to match them. If you are working with a napped fabric such as velvet, be sure the nap is running smooth downwards and to the front. Be sure to mark top and bottom on all of the pieces you cut. Sometimes even a plain fabric should be cut with all the pieces running in the same direction to insure the same color shading.

The first step when putting your chair back together will be the deck area. Make center marks on the front and back of your chair frame. When the fabric is applied, all centered patterns and stripes should line up with these marks. These measurements must be exact! If your center marks are not correct, all the patterns or stripes will be off center and will not match properly. To cut out the deck using a patterned fabric you need to determine where on the fabric to start cutting. You already have determined what pattern will be centered from the centered pattern on the cushion top. You will need to work **backwards** to determine the flow of the pattern from the front of the cushion top, down to the boxing on the cushion and then down to the deck (Figure 12-8). If you are applying a skirt to your chair, the pattern should match and follow down from the deck area. When looking at the front of the completed chair, the pattern should flow from the bottom all the way up the front of the chair, and to the cushion top. This is not hard to do if you know *All the Trade Secrets.*

To make the deck match and flow to the boxing of the cushion, start at the center of your cushion top. In most cases, you will cut the deck from the center pattern on the fabric. The deck will be approximately 40″ to 50″ in width. If you start marking on a side pattern, you would not have enough fabric on one side to cut the deck in its entirety. Place your old cushion on the chair and imagine your pattern flowing from the cushion top, to the bottom of the chair. The front of the deck needs to match the boxing on the front of the cushion. To do this, roll out your fabric and find the pattern in the **center** of the fabric that will be used as the center of your cushion. Place a chalk mark in the center of this pattern (Figure 12-9). From this point determine how many inches it is to the front of the cushion. Measure down that distance on the fabric and make additional chalk marks at this point and strike a chalk line. This chalk line is the front of the cushion (Figure 12-10). Next, measure the height of the cushion boxing. Let's say it is 4″ thick. From your last chalk marks (which was the front of the cushion) you would measure down another 4″ or whatever thickness your cushion boxing actually is (Figure 12-11). Make these chalk marks a little bolder than the last chalk marks. At this point remove the cushion from your chair. Measure from the front of the deck to where it meets and is sewn to the decking material. This measurement will be approximately 4″ to 6″. This area is called the setback (Figure 12-12). Transfer your setback measurement to the fabric. From the bold chalk line, measure upwards

Figure 12-13

Figure 12-14

Figure 12-15

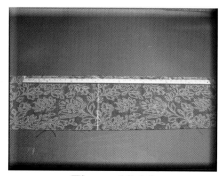

Figure 12-16

the distance of your setback plus 1/2″ for a seam allowance. Keeping the pattern straight, mark this area with chalk and strike a line from selvage to selvage (Figure 12-13). The selvages are the edges of the fabric and normally cut off when cutting out your fabric. This is where you will be making your first cut. This is the top of the decking piece you will cut. Cut the decking from top to bottom to the appropriate height. You should have these measurements already recorded. Starting at the center of the pattern, measure outwards on each side and cut the width of the decking fabric (Figure 12-14). You will now have a large rectangular shaped piece of fabric. At this point you can either use your old deck as a pattern, or cut the new deck from the measurements of the chair. If you do decide to use your old deck as a pattern, remember to fold it in half and make a small clip in the center of fabric, on the top edge. This will be your center and should line up with the center on the new decking fabric you just cut.

To cut the decking fabric for a T-shaped cushion, you will need to miter the corners. Begin by measuring from corner to corner on the chairs deck area (Figure 12-15). Working from the center of the deck fabric you just cut, transfer this measurement making sure you have equal halves marked out. Place chalk marks at the top edge (Figure 12-16). Measure the setback and transfer that measurement to the top edge of the deck fabric just below the chalk marks that you made to indicate the corners (Figure 12-17). You will now measure downwards from the top edge of the fabric at these chalk marks. Measure down the distance of your setback. For example, if your setback is 5″ deep, you will measure down from the top edge 5″. If your setback were 4″, you would measure down 4″. Measure down the distance of your setback and make a chalk mark at this point. Working from the marks on the top of the fabric that you made to indicate the corners, measure outwards on both sides of the chalk mark the same distance as your setback measurement. If your setback is 5″ you will measure from the chalk mark that indicated your corner, 5″ in each direction (Figure 12-18). Connect these marks to form a triangular shape. Repeat this step on the other side of the fabric. This triangular shape will be the **finished size** of the miter. You will cut 1/2″ inside the lines you just marked. The 1/2″ will be the seam allowance (Figure 12-19). You should now have a rectangular piece of fabric with two triangles cut out on the top edge (Figure 12-20). *Tip!* If you are working with a striped fabric, after the first triangular cut is made, fold the deck at the center, line up the stripes and use the first triangular cut out as a pattern for the second cut out. This will save you a little time and ensure that both corners are mirror images (Figure 12-21).

To sew the mitered corners, fold the fabric face to face at one of the triangular cut outs. Keep the two diagonally cut edges of the triangle together and the two top edges together. Starting from the top edge, sew

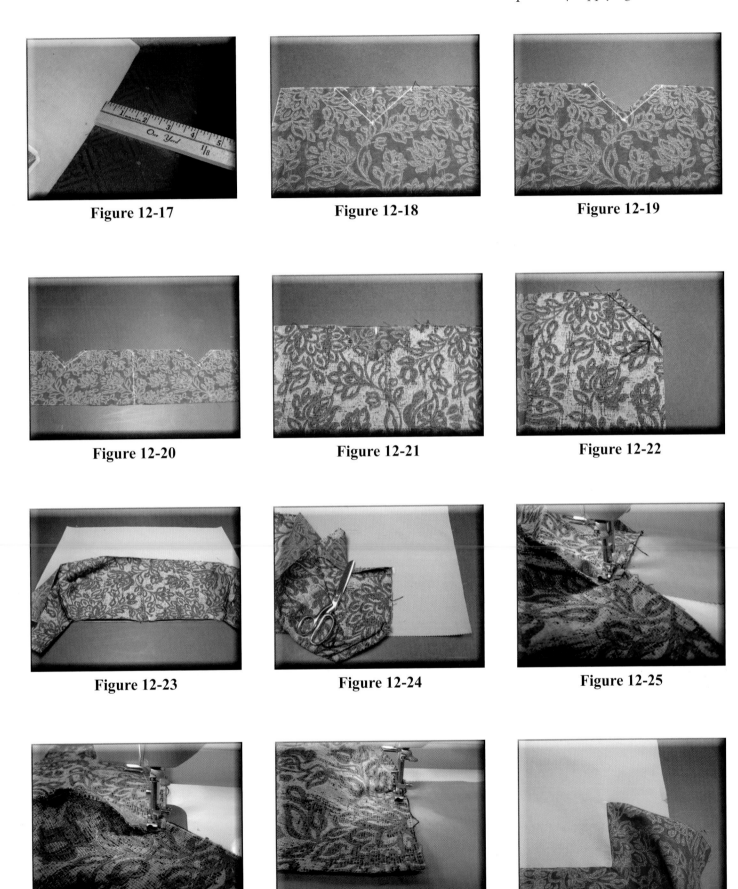

Figure 12-17

Figure 12-18

Figure 12-19

Figure 12-20

Figure 12-21

Figure 12-22

Figure 12-23

Figure 12-24

Figure 12-25

Figure 12-26

Figure 12-27

Figure 12-28

Figure 12-29

Figure 12-30

Figure 12-31

Figure 12-32

downwards towards the pointed edge. *Tip!* Instead of sewing a straight line, curve the very tip to create a slight curve on the corners of the deck. If you were to sew a straight line, the corners of the deck would be pointed instead of slightly rounded. Repeat this step on the other triangular cut out (Figure 12-22). Fit the sewn deck onto the chair. It should have a snug fit.

Sew the decking material onto the deck fabric or denim you have just cut and sewn. Cut the decking material large enough to allow for pulling and stapling. Fold the front edge of the decking material in half and make a small notch in the fabric to indicate the center. Do not make this notch too large. You only have a 1/2″ seam allowance to work with. With the decking fabric facing inwards, line up the two notches and pin to hold in place (Figure 12-23). Pull the decking fabric across the front of the decking material. Keep the edges straight and work from the center to the **right** side of the decking fabric. When you reach the sew line from the mitered corner, make a few small clips in the fabric to help turn the fabric to form a 90° angle. Pin this area after the decking fabric has been folded back to form a 90° angle. There should be approximately 4″–8″ of fabric remaining from the sew line. Follow the fabric back keeping it parallel to the edge of the decking material. Fold the last 1/2″ of fabric under and pin this to the decking material. This will be top stitched to the decking fabric later (Figure 12-24). Start sewing at the folded end and continue sewing to the mitered corner sew line. Make a 90° turn and continue sewing along the front edge keeping the two edges of fabric even (Figures 12-25 & 26). Continue sewing until the other side is completed (Figure 12-27). *Tip!* Keep the needle of the sewing machine in the down position when turning a corner and repositioning your fabric. By keeping the needle in the down position it helps pin the material together. The folded edges on both sides of the decking where you started and finished sewing will now be top stitched to the decking material (Figure 12-28). To top stitch the fabric, simply lay the folded decking fabric over the decking material. Stitch the two pieces together along the folded edge (Figures 12-29 & 30). The completed decking can now be hand sewn onto the deck area (Figure 12-31).

Place a center mark on the deck area where the old deck was hand sewn into place. This should be at the edge of your setback. If you are working with new burlap over the springs, measure the depth of the setback and strike a straight line across the burlap at the proper depth. Line up the notches with the center mark on the deck (Figure 12-32). Using nylon button twine and a curved needle, hand-sew the sewn decking fabrics to the burlap.

With the front of the chair facing you, staple the button twine onto the side of the side frame rail at the point it is to be hand sewn. Flip-flop the end of the button twine while stapling. This will make the twine

Figure 12-33

Figure 12-34

Figure 12-35

Figure 12-36

very secure. With the other end of the button twine through the eye of the curved needle, place the end of the needle through the two layers of fabric and then through the burlap (Figure 12-32). Bring the tip of the curved needle upwards through the burlap approximately 1-1/2″ from the point you entered the burlap. Bring the tip of the curved needle through the decking material and the decking fabric that is sewn together and continue sewing. Space the stitches approximately 1-1/2″ apart. When you finish hand sewing, pull the twine very tight. Staple the end of the twine flip flopping the twine while stapling.

If you are reusing the padding on the deck area, you can add a layer of cotton to the existing padding. If you elect to put new padding on the deck area, cut a piece of deck pad a little larger than the deck area. The ends of the pad will be tucked under the bottom of the arms. Place the edge of the deck pad along the sewn line and trim the remaining three sides to fit. The other three sides should tuck under the inside arms and the inside back. Leave enough space to staple the decking material to the top of the rail. Place strips of cotton padding under the deck pad on these three sides. This will help to close the gap between the deck and the inside arms and the inside back. Pull the decking material under the back rail and loose tack it in the center. Continue loose tacking the back starting from the center and stopping short of the back legs. Re-stretch the decking material and staple it into place stopping a few inches from the back legs. Cut the decking material on the sides of the chair next. You will cut around the arm post on each side. *Tip!* I like to use a regulator to help mark out where the cuts will be made (Figures 12-33 through 35). Fold the top stitched area of the deck back and up to the arm post. As opposed to cutting perpendicular to the arm post, cut the fabric with a slight angle approximately 3″ – 4″ back from perpendicular. This will allow you extra fabric to be pulled around the front of the arm post. Cut to the center of the post and stop just short of the post. Make a Y style cut and pull the decking material under the side rails and loose tack (Figures 12-36 through 38). To cut around the back legs, fold the decking material towards the center of the deck area and cut from this point to the front of the back leg (Figures 12-39 & 40). Finish stapling the deck area and repeat this process on the other side (Figures 12-41 & 42). The next step is to pad the front edge of the deck area.

There will be several layers of cotton used to pad the front edge of the deck. If the front edge does not have an edge roll, install one at this point. The first layer of cotton will start at the hand sewn line and continue to the beginning of the edge roll. The second layer of cotton will start in the same place but continue to the center of the edge roll. The third layer of cotton will start in the same place again and continue over the edges of the edge roll. The fourth layer of cotton will extend a few inches further. Pull the deck fabric over the cotton padding. Be sure to push the cotton back into place when pulling the fabric. Start

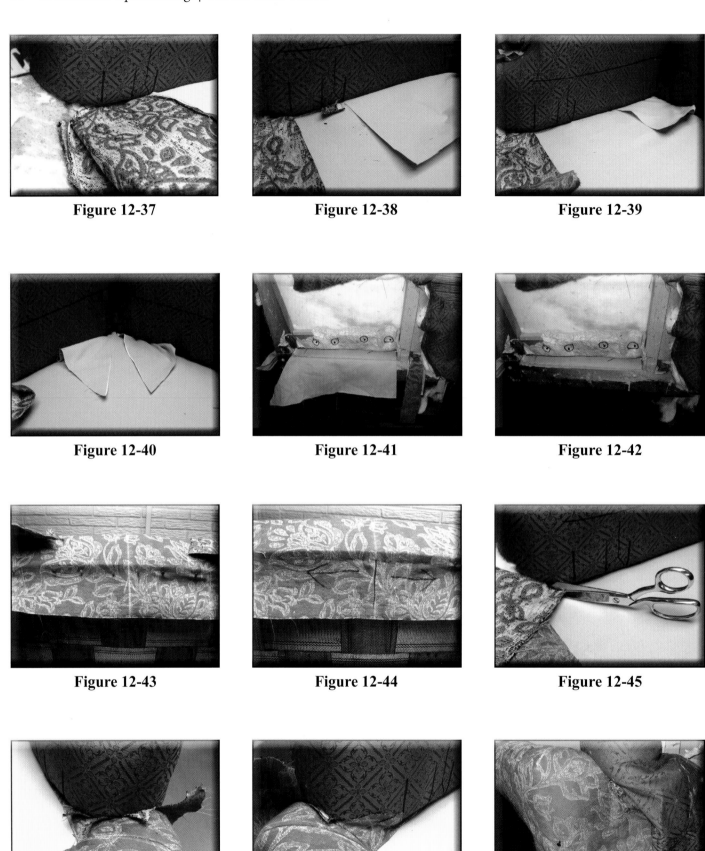

Figure 12-37

Figure 12-38

Figure 12-39

Figure 12-40

Figure 12-41

Figure 12-42

Figure 12-43

Figure 12-44

Figure 12-45

Figure 12-46

Figure 12-47

Figure 12-48

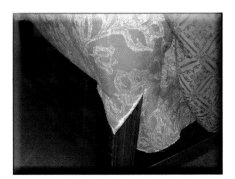

Figure 12-49

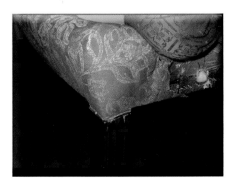

Figure 12-50

Figure 12-51

Figure 12-52

loose tacking the fabric by aligning the center marks on the frame and on the fabric. Loose tack the deck fabric from the center outwards (Figure 12-43). Make sure the cotton padding does not extend over the bottom edge. A welt cord trim or skirt will be applied later in this area. Keep the cotton padding about 1″ from the bottom edge. Stapling the cotton padding in place can be helpful. After re-stretching the fabric a few times, staple the deck into place stopping short of the front legs (Figure 12-44). Finish cutting around the front of the arms by making small cuts to help the fabric pivot around the front of the arms. The raw edges of the fabric can be tucked in with the help of a regulator (Figures 12-45 through 48).

Cut around the front legs by cutting the fabric from the center of the leg at the bottom to where the inside corner of the leg meets the bottom of the front and side rails (Figure 12-49). Make these cuts on both of the legs. Fold the raw edges under and staple the remaining fabric (Figure 12-50). If you are adding a skirt on the chair, staple the fabric on the very bottom edge of the rails and not underneath. You will not have to cut around the front leg. The skirt will cover the staples. Loose tack the ends of the deck for now. During the process of installing the outside arms, the ends of the deck will be stapled into place (Figures 12-51 & 52).

Section B: Inside Arms

Tip! When applying fabric to the inside arms, always repeat the same step to the opposite arm at the same time. If you make a cut on one arm, immediately make the same cut on the other arm. This will speed the cutting process and ensure exact matching of the pattern from one arm to the other. The inside arms should be the mirror image of each other when completed. *Tip!* It would be to your advantage to remove the padding on the inside back before you upholster the inside arms and inside wings. It is much easier to see where to make your cuts if the padding has been removed. Sometimes it is worth the additional steps and time to remove the inside back padding and then reinstall it later (Figure 12-53).

Loose tack the top of the arm making sure you have enough fabric to wrap around the front of the arm and enough fabric to wrap around the back of the chair (Figure 12-54). At this time make sure your stripes are straight or your pattern has been centered properly. If you are working with a napped fabric, the nap should be running smooth downwards. *Tip!* Make sure your pattern is properly centered from the top of the arm to the top of the cushion. Place the cushion into the chair and center your pattern. *Tip!* Do not center the pattern from the top of the arm to the top of the deck. Once you are pleased with the positioning of

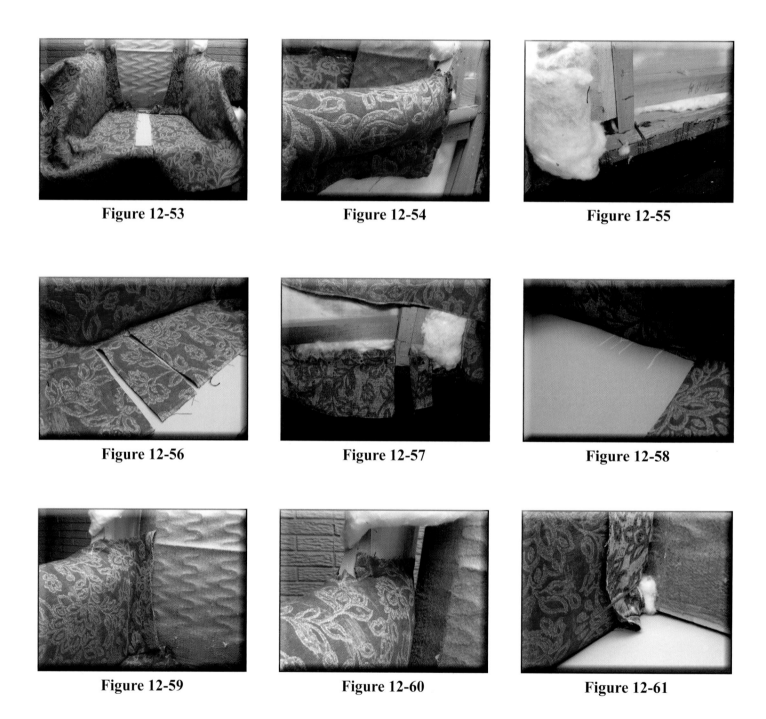

Figure 12-53

Figure 12-54

Figure 12-55

Figure 12-56

Figure 12-57

Figure 12-58

Figure 12-59

Figure 12-60

Figure 12-61

Figure 12-62

Figure 12-63

Figure 12-64

your stripes or patterns, cut around the arm posts. Fold the fabric back until the fold is in the front of the arm post. Place the flat end of the regulator next to the arm post to use as a guide to cut the fabric (Figure 12-55). Cut the fabric next to the regulator. This cut should be perpendicular to the arm post. Stop the cut approximately 1″ short of the post and end the cut with a Y shaped cut. Re-tighten the fabric and staple the top and bottom (Figures 12-56 through 58). Stop stapling just short of the front arm post and the back stretcher rail. If you are working on a wing chair, you will stop stapling just short of the front of the wing post. Make a cut along the top of the arm and aim for the center of the wing post. Stop the cut approximately 1″ short of the post. From this point, make a cut on one side of the wing and then the other side of the wing. This cut should look like the letter Y (Figures 12-59 & 60). Do not make these cuts too deep. You can always cut a little deeper later if needed. Loose tack the bottom of the wing and the front of the arm now and continue by working on the back of the inside arm. The fabric will now be vertically folded back and stop just in front of the back stretcher rail. Place the regulator between the back stretcher post and the back leg post (Figure 12-61). Slide the regulator down until you reach the top of the back stretcher rail. This is the rail you need to cut around next. With the regulator in place, make another Y styled cut up to the back stretcher rail. Push the top portion of the fabric through the rail and loose tack the fabric on the inside of the back rail (Figures 12-62 & 63). The fabric will be stapled later on the inside of the rail, as opposed to the outside because this would create unnecessary bulk on the back rail. This is the same reason you try to staple on the top of the side rails as opposed to the sides of the rails. The bottom portion of the fabric will be folded back and cut around the back leg. Fold the bottom portion of fabric keeping the fold just in front of the back leg, this should form a point in the front of the fabric. From this point, cut the fabric to the front of the back leg. Push the back half of fabric under the stretcher rail and through to the back. The other half of the cut will go under the side stretcher rail and be loose tacked (Figure 12-64). *Tip!* You know you cut the fabric deep enough if you can pull on one side of the fabric and the other side of the fabric does not move around the leg. Now that all of the fabric has been loose tacked into place, staple all of the fabric into place in the same order that you loose tacked. **Do not staple the back corner on the sides yet.** *Tip!* Always remember when tacking or stapling, staple the top and bottom, then side to side. This will insure an even stretch on the fabric and will keep the stripes or patterned fabric straight. To complete the front of the arms, make small cuts to let the fabric pivot around the front of the arm. Loose tack the front of the arm. Make small relief cuts to let the fabric curve around the rounded arms (Figure 12-65). Re-stretch the fabric and staple the fabric in place (Figure 12-66). The pleats will be done last. Make small pleats on the arm fronts. Remember to cut out the bulk when making the pleats

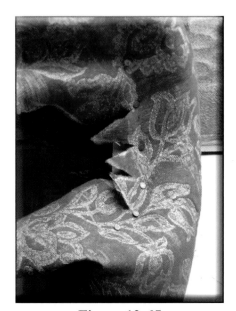

Figure 12-65

Figure 12-66

(Figure 12-67). There are several styles of arm fronts. Make the front of the arms in the same manner that they were made originally.

Section C: Inside Wings

The inside wings will be the next step. Place a yardstick along the bottom edge of the fabric you have cut for the inside wing. Keep the bottom edge of the yardstick even with the bottom edge of the fabric. Strike a chalk line along the top edge of the yardstick. Determine if this is the left or the right facing inside wing. You will be cutting a slight curve on the bottom edge at the front of the fabric to help it curve around the front of the wing. This also helps in preventing any gaps where the fabric will meet the inside arm. If the fabric was cut straight across the bottom and stapled into place there would be a gap at the end of the wing where it meets the top of the inside arm (Figure 12-68). This curve will be on the outside edges at the bottom of the wings. Measure inwards approximately 3″ from the outside bottom edges and make a chalk mark on the bottom outside edge. Draw a gradual curve to the chalk mark you just made. Cut the fabric on the chalk line at the bottom of the fabric making sure to cut the curve in the bottom of the wing (Figure 12-69). Place this cut inside wing fabric face to face and on top of the other inside wing fabric. You will use this as a pattern to cut the opposite wing (Figure 12-70). Welt cord will now be sewn onto the bottom of each inside wing (Figure 12-71). Some inside wing fabrics are applied with cardboard tacking strip, machine sewn directly to the inside arm, or in most cases, hand sewn to the inside arm (Figure 12-72). Place the inside wing fabric with the welt cord machine sewn at the bottom over the inside arm. If you have a stripe or a patterned fabric you need to match, move the welt cord forward or backwards to match the pattern. Loose tack the welt cord in the back of the chair and on the side of the back rail. Pull the welt cord over the front of the wing and loose tack to the outside of the wing. Hand sew the welt cord to the inside arms now. *Tip!* Make sure the welt cords are tacked in the back at the same height. To do this, measure with your yardstick from the bottom of the back rail to the center of the welt cord (Figure 12-73). The measurement should be the same on both sides. Pull the fabric over the top of the wing and loose tack. *Tip!* If you have a striped fabric, place a yardstick towards the back of the arm and vertically from the deck to the top of the inside wing. This line can be used as a gauge to keep a stripe straight and matched from the wing to the arm. Make adjustments to the stripe if needed now (Figure 12-74). Once the top has been loose tacked and the fabric has been re-stretched and loose tacked again, staple the top area of the inside wing. Stop short of the curve area in the front of the wing and a few inches from the back. Fold the fabric in the back of the wing so that it is parallel to the inside back. Using your regulator again, place a flat side

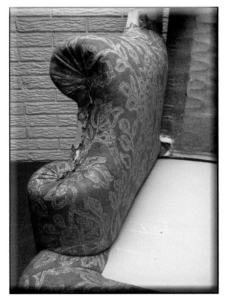

Figure 12-67

Figure 12-68

Figure 12-69

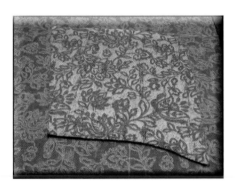

Figure 12-70

Figure 12-71

Figure 12-72

Figure 12-73

Figure 12-74

Figure 12-75

Figure 12-76

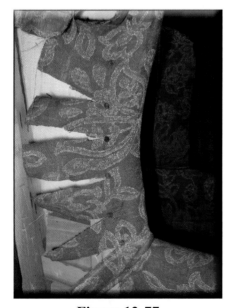

Figure 12-77

under the back rail and hold it level. Cut along this line and cut only as deep as needed to be able to pull the material through the back and not have the cut marks show (Figure 12-75). Pull the fabric through the rail and loose tack it to the inside back leg post. Be careful not to pull the fabric too tight. This can cause the patterned or striped fabric to bow (Figure 12-76). Starting from the welt cord in the front of the wing, pull the fabric tightly towards the top smoothing the fabric as you go. Loose tack the fabric on the outside of the wing near the top. Again starting from the welt cord, pull the fabric taunt and loose tack. You may have to make small relief cuts into the fabric on the inside curved areas when loose tacking up the side of the wing. Be careful not to pull the fabric too tight. This can cause a stripe to bow. A relief cut is a small cut that is made into an area such as the inside curve of a wing. These small cuts provide the fabric with a little more stretch that it may need to conform to a curved area (Figure 12-77). Make very tiny pleats on the outside of the wing. Start from the bottom of the curve on the front of the wing. Continue loose tacking the pleats until all of the fabric has been completely pleated on the curve. You will now go back to the area where you made a cut near the top of the rail. This is where you pulled the fabric through to the back. Fold the material back keeping the fold parallel to the inside back. Make a diagonal cut to the top of the back rail. Do not make this cut too deep. The balance of the fabric on the top of the wing should be easily folded over the top rail now. The triangular piece that was just cut can be stapled to the frame or tucked under the padding on the inside back (Figure 12-78). Continuing on the outside top of the wing by folding the fabric around to the back of the chair and then fold the fabric from the top over. *Tip!* When making a fold or pleat, think about dust settling into this area. You always want the folds or the pleats going downwards if possible. Once the inside wing has been loose tacked into place, retrace your steps, stapling the fabric into place. (Figures 12-79 & 80).

Section D: Inside Back

Before upholstering the inside back of the chair determine if you are going to use the original padding. If you have removed the inside back padding before upholstering the inside arms and the inside wings, you can reattach it now or replace it with new padding. If you are going to reuse the old padding, or use new padding, add a layer of polyester or cotton padding (Figure 12-81). Trim the padding to fit under the bottom rail and not over the top rail. Cut the sides a little wider so they tuck around the old padding. Make sure the top of the padding does not come over the top rail. This area should remain smooth because a welt cord trim will be applied on the top edge later. Make sure you have the centers marked on the top and the bottom of the frame and on

Figure 12-78

Figure 12-79

Figure 12-80

Figure 12-81

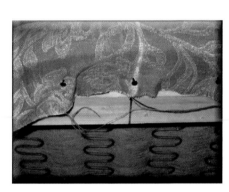

Figure 12-82

Figure 12-83

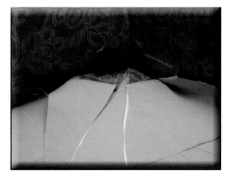

Figure 12-84

Figure 12-85

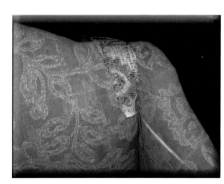

Figure 12-86

Figure 12-87

the fabric. Lay the fabric over the padding and loose tack the top edge leaving a few inches to pull later (Figure 12-82). Be sure to match any pattern from side to side now. This would be a pattern such as a plaid. Starting from the center, lining up the center marks on the chair to the fabric. Push the fabric through the bottom rail and center the pattern. Loose tack the bottom stopping short of the legs. **Do not tuck the sides in yet!** Re-stretch the fabric on the top and bottom and staple into place stopping short of the legs and the top edges. You will cut the inside back fabric around the structure rails in the same manner the inside arm and inside wings were cut. Use the same Y style cut to cut the fabric at the bottom rail (Figure 12-83). You will also fold the bottom fabric at the leg and cut from the point to the leg. Each raw edge will be folded under. One half of the fabric is being pulled to the back rail, and the other half is being pulled to the side rail (Figure 12-84). After you staple the bottom corner on the side rail, finish stapling the corner of the arm you did not staple earlier (Figure 12-85). At the top cut, after the fabric has been pulled through the rail and loose tacked, fold the remaining top fabric vertically to the inside wing and trim the fabric leaving approximately 1″ remaining (Figure 12-86). Fold under the remaining 1″ of fabric and tuck it behind the padding. Pull tightly over the top edge, and staple into place. Repeat this step on the other side to complete the inside back (Figure 12-87). *Tip!* Stuff a small amount of cotton or polyester batting where the top of the inside arm and the inside wing meet. This is done in the back and though the back stretcher post and the back leg post. This is where you pulled the fabric through and stapled to the inside rail. Use the flat side of your regulator and gently push the padding to close the gap in this area. Look at the front of the chair as you are stuffing to make sure you are using the proper amount. By doing this, it fills in the gap and gives a much more professional look (Figure 12-88).

Section E: Outside Wings / Outside Arms

To begin upholstering the outsides of the chair, place the chair on its side. It is always easier to work downwards. Staple a welt cord from the top of the outside back along the edge of the outside wing and finishing under the outside arm. Be sure to cut the rope out of the welt cord on the top edge before stapling to avoid bulk. Fold this edge towards the bottom and keep the welt cord centered on the edge of the frame when stapling the welt cord on the outside wing. Pli-grip will be stapled to the welted area. The pli-grip should not extend under the arm (Figures 12-89 & 90). *Tip!* When stapling pli-grip, always start with a full section. By this I mean start with the factory curved edge and not a cut edge. Masking tape can be applied to the edges to make the edges less sharp. This is normally done when using a very lightweight fabric and on corners. Start stapling the pli-grip at the top of the outside wing.

Figure 12-88

Figure 12-89

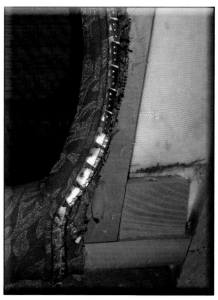

Figure 12-90

Keep the straight side with the hole in it pressed tightly up against the welt cord. One leg of the staple should be stapled into each hole. Determine the length of pli-grip needed and precut that length, as opposed to stapling to the end and then trying to cut off the end piece. Push the edges of the pli-grip a little more than half of the way down. Cut polyester batting or cotton and staple it up to the edge of the pli-grip and to the edges of the back and bottom of the outside wing. This will make a nicely padded surface (Figure 12-91). *Tip!* It is easier to precut the batting before stapling it into place. It is very difficult to trim the batting once it is stapled into place. Burlap may be added before applying the polyester or cotton batting to form a more solid base on all outside areas. If you had a plain fabric the outside wing would be installed now. If you are matching a pattern, fold the top edge of the outside arm fabric under approximately 1″ and place it under the top of the outside arm. Continue over the wing area, around the back, making sure to have enough in the front to staple or pli-grip to finish the edge. If you are matching a stripe or centering a pattern, slide the fabric from side to side, allowing the patterns to match. Flip the fabric up and put a few loose tacks under the arm to hold the fabric in place. Pull the fabric back down and loose tack on the bottom of the chair and a few on the outside back. Place your outside wing fabric on top of the wing area. Shift the fabric until it matches up to the outside arm. *Tip!* If you are using a striped fabric, place a yardstick vertically over the stripes on the outside arm. This line will help you continue the stripe on the outside wing. By following the edge of the yardstick, you can match the wing fabric and keep the stripe straight to the top of the wing. When this is completed, the fabric will be installed into the pli-grip. Staple the bottom of the wing into place keeping the staples low enough to let the arm fabric cover them later. With the pointed side of your regulator, push the fabric into place at the top of the wing. The small teeth on the inside lip of the pli-grip will grab and hold the fabric. Slide the regulator from the center to the ends. You should see the fabric beginning to tighten now (Figure 12-92). Again, just on the top edge, push down on the lip of the pli-grip with your thumb. This helps to lock the fabric into place. Smooth the fabric around the back of the chair and staple into place. Be sure not to pull the fabric too tightly causing the fabric to bow. Tuck the fabric into the opposite side now just like you did on the top. You may have to make small relief cuts in the fabric (Figure 12-93). When all the pli-grip has been pushed down with your thumb, trim off the excess fabric very close to the edge of the pli-grip (Figure 12-94). With the pointed side of the regulator, push the excess fabric into the gap by sliding the regulator along the edges (Figure 12-95). Once this step has been completed on all of the sides, tap the edge of the pli-grip with your tack hammer just below the welt cord. Tap firmly, but not hard enough to cut the fabric (Figure 12-96). The outside wing has now been completed (Figure 12-97). Flip up the outside arm fabric and place a few staples under the arm to hold the fabric in place. Apply

Figure 12-91

Figure 12-92

Figure 12-93

Figure 12-94

cardboard tack strip under the arm, keeping the edge of the tack strip straight and along the edge of the arm and over the outside wing (Figure 12-98). Staple polyester batting along all the edges of the outside arm (Figure 12-99). Pull the fabric over the bottom edge of the chair. Make sure to keep any stripe or patterned fabric straight. Staple the fabric in place stopping short of the legs. This process is called blind tacking. To cut around the back leg, pull the fabric taut and cut from the back of the leg to the inside corner of the leg (Figures 12-100 & 101). Fold the excess fabric under and staple into place. Repeat this step if you are cutting around a front leg. Your chair may have pli-grip on the front edge or may have the fabric folded under and stapled on the bottom. Some arm fronts will be covered with an arm panel.

Section F: Outside Back

Welt cord will be applied to the outside back of the chair much like the outside wings. The ends of the welt cord will need to be finished. To finish the end, cut approximately 1-1/2″ of the stitches out of the welt. Cut the rope off and fold approximately 3/4″ of fabric over to cover the raw end (Figure 12-102). Place this finished end at the top of the back leg and staple in place. Continue stapling the welt cord. Make sure to center the welt cord on the edge of the frame. Finish the opposite end of the welt cord just like the first side (Figure 12-103). Staple on the sew lines of the welt cord. If the top of the outside back of your chair is straight and not rounded, you can use cardboard tack strip on this top edge to apply the fabric. This will be done just like the outside arms. If cardboard tack strip is being used on the top edge, this will be the first step and the bottom will be the second step. If the outside back has a curved or rounded top, use pli-grip to secure the fabric to the top edge. Apply the pli-grip to the sides and then staple polyester batting to the outside back (Figure 12-104). Lay the outside back fabric over the back of the chair and staple the bottom starting from center (Figure 12-105). Match any patterns to the outside arms at this time. Pull the fabric to the top starting in the center and lock it into place with pli-grip. Finish pli-gripping the top (Figures 12-106 & 107), and continue by completing the sides (Figures 12-108 & 109). Cut the fabric around the back leg in the same manner as the outside arm was cut (Figure 12-110). Cardboard tack strip with tacks can be used to apply the fabric to the sides of the outside back if it is straight. Pli-grip must be used if the sides are curved. To use the tack strip, place the cardboard strip next to the side of the outside back (Figure 12-111), and push the tacks through the fabric (Figure 12-112), and trim off the extra fabric. Turn the tack strip over and tap it into place along the welt cord with a mallet or a tack hammer. Be careful not to damage the fabric.

Figure 12-95

Figure 12-96

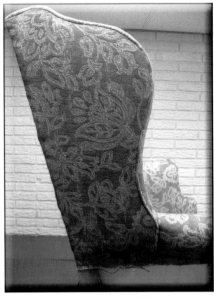

Figure 12-97

Figure 12-98

Figure 12-99

Figure 12-100

Figure 12-101

Figure 12-102

Figure 12-103

Figure 12-104

Figure 12-105

Figure 12-106

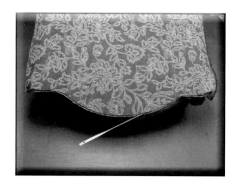

Figure 12-107

Figure 12-108

Figure 12-109

Figure 12-110

Figure 12-111

Figure 12-112

Figure 12-113

Figure 12-114

Figure 12-115

Figure 12-116

Section G: Base Welt Trim

Place the chair upside down with the legs facing upwards. A welt cord will be stapled on the bottom of the chair frame to provide a finished look. This is called a base welt trim. Measure around the base of the chair and add a few inches. Cut a piece of welt cord to this length and make sure not to have a seam on the front edge. Remember to look for the extra tail on the welt to easily find the seams. Plug in your hot glue gun at this time. While the glue gun is heating up, start stapling the welt cord in the back of the chair. Leave a few inches at the end not stapled (Figure 12-113). Staple along the back and on the sew line of the welt. Stop short of the back leg and neatly trim out the excess fabric on the tail of the welt cord to fit around the leg. Trim as close to the sew line as possible (Figure 12-114). Place a bead of hot glue at the edge of the fabric over the leg and apply the welt cord over this area (Figure 12-115). Continue this process and finish the welt cord in the back. Finish the welt cord by cutting one length approximately 2″ longer than the other (Figure 12-116). Cut the threads out of the longer welt cord. Cut the rope to butt up against the other end of the welt (Figure 12-117). Fold approximately 1/2″ of the raw edge under and overlap the other welt and staple into position (Figures 12-118 & 119).

Section H: Cambric

Cambric is the black dust cover applied on the bottom of the chair to give it a finished look. Cut the cambric approximately 4″ larger from front to back and from side to side. Working from the back to the front, fold under the raw edges and staple from the center outwards. Staple on the sew lines of the welt cord and stop short of the corners. Repeat this step on the sides of the chair (Figure 12-120). To cut around the legs, fold the cambric back keeping the fold on the corner of the leg (Figure 12-121). This should form a point on the opposite side. Cut from this point to the inside corner of the leg. Trim any excess fabric, fold the raw edges under and staple into place (Figure 12-122).

Figure 12-117

Figure 12-118

Figure 12-119

Figure 12-120

Figure 12-121

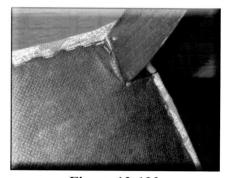

Figure 12-122

Chapter 13 | Arm Panels

Figure 13-1

Figure 13-2

Arm panels are normally made out of very heavy weight cardboard because it can be cut and shaped to conform to the odd shapes of the arms (Figure 13-1). These panels are padded and covered with fabric and used to hide the raw edges of fabric on the front of the arms (Figure 13-2). Welt cord can be added to the panels for a more professional appearance (Figures 13-3 & 4). The arm panels are attached to the frame with the use of finish nails or panel nails. Finish nails are very thin and have a tiny head (Figure 13-5). The finish nail is hammered through the fabric-covered panel to secure it to the frame. The head of the nail can be covered when a regulator is used to lift the fabric over the head of the nail (Figures 13-6 & 7). Only fabric with an open weave should be applied with finish nails. If you are working with a finely woven fabric, vinyl, or leather, panel nails must be used to secure the panels to the frame. Panel nails have a washer attached to a nail. The washer keeps the nail in place (Figure 13-8). The panel nails are hammered through the cardboard then the cardboard is padded and covered with fabric (Figure 13-9). The upholstered panels can be applied with a mallet or a tack hammer (Figures 13-10 & 11).

Figure 13-3

Figure 13-4

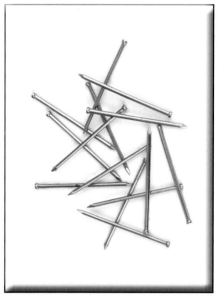

Figure 13-5

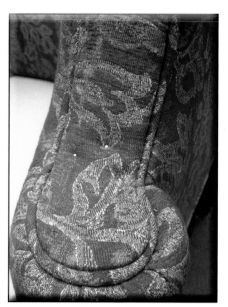

Figure 13-6

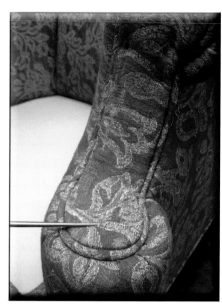

Figure 13-7

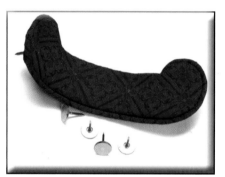

Figure 13-8

Figure 13-9

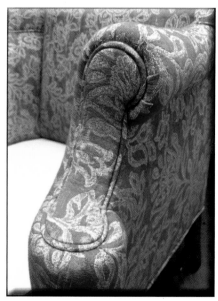

Figure 13-10

Figure 13-11

Chapter 14 | Cutting Cushions and Pillows with a Crown

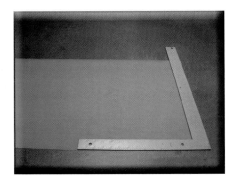

Figure 14-1

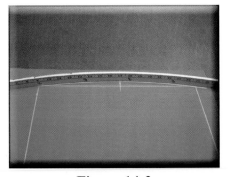

Figure 14-2

If your cushions or throw pillows will have a lot of loft or plumpness, you will have to cut the covers with a crown. Picture a very square throw pillow. Now install a very puffy pillow core. The sewn edges will bow inwards. The more loft the pillow has, the more the edges will bow inwards. *Tip!* To prevent this bowing from happening, mark out the square shape of your pillow with chalk (Figure 14-1). Measure upwards approximately 1/2″–3/4″ in the center of one of the edges. Chalk this measurement in the center of the pillow. Using a yardstick and possibly someone else's help, bend the yardstick from corner to corner. Bow the center of the yardstick to connect your chalk mark you just made (Figures 14-2 & 3). Repeat this step on the other three sides before cutting. *Tip!* You can fold the already marked side to the opposite side and use it as a pattern. This will eliminate having to bow the yardstick on the other side (Figure 14-4). By cutting the fabric with a crown the four sides of the pillow will be very straight when stuffed with a lofty filling. This is also true of cushions used with furniture. Back cushions tend to have more of a crown then seat cushions because they are normally more lofted. When you see a seat or back cushion in a chair follow the pattern from corner to corner. If the cover was cut with a crown there will be more of the pattern showing in the center area of the cushion face.

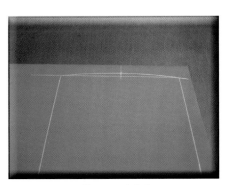

Figure 14-3

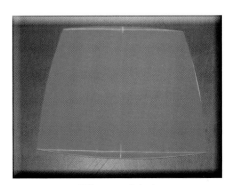

Figure 14-4

Chapter 15 | Cushion Making

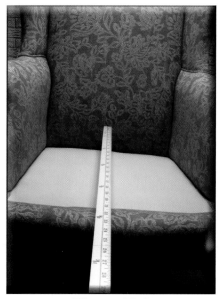

Figure 15-1

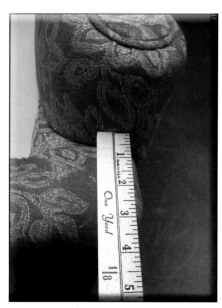

Figure 15-2

It is always best to construct the cushions last. If the old cushions are used as a pattern they will most likely not fit the newly upholstered chair properly. The measurements of your chair can change when using all new fillings or the addition of new padding to the existing padding. Pulling and stretching the new fabric tighter than the old fabric will also cause the inside arms and the front to back measurements of the seat to be altered. The best time to make the cushion is to wait until the chair has been completed. Draw out the shape of the cushion on paper. If the cushion is square shaped, draw out a square. If your cushion is T shaped, draw the T shape on paper.

To measure the cushion you will need a yardstick and a flexible tape measure. *Tip!* Determine the thickness of your cushion and record this measurement. Using your yardstick, measure up from the deck and make a chalk mark on both inside arms at the height of your cushion. If your cushion measures 4″, you will measure up 4″ and place a mark on both inside arms at this point. Measure the side-to-side area later with a tape measure. Still using your yardstick, measure up from the deck and place a chalk mark on the inside back. Measure from this point on the inside back, to the front edge of the deck (Figure 15-1). This is your finished front to back measurement of the cushion. Record this measurement on your drawing. Next you will measure the T area. Using your yardstick, measure from the front of the arms to the front of the deck and record this measurement on your drawing (Figure 15-2). Measure across the front of the deck to determine the width of the cushion at the T area (Figure 15-3). Record this measurement on your drawing. Now you will use your flexible tape measure for the following measurements. Measuring from the chalk marks you previously made on the inside arms, measure from inside arm to inside arm (Figure 15-4). Record these measurements on your drawing. Measure the inside arms again moving up towards the front of the arms where the T shape begins (Figure 15-5). Record this measurement on your drawing. It is quite common for this measurement to be larger than the back of the cushion. *Tip!* In most cases the inside back of the chair is not perfectly straight across the back. There will be a slight curve on the ends of the inside back where the fabric has been pulled tightly. You will need to add this curve to let the back of the cushion hug the inside back of the chair. To do this, mark a line approximately 3/4″ longer on each side

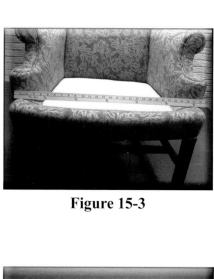

Figure 15-3

Figure 15-4

Figure 15-5

Figure 15-6

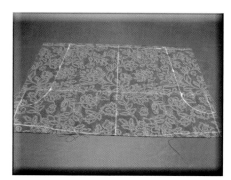

Figure 15-7

Figure 15-8

Figure 15-9

Figure 15-10

Figure 15-11

Figure 15-12

Figure 15-13

Figure 15-14

Figure 15-15

of the back corners of the cushion. Gradually curve a line from that point, towards the center of the cushion. You do not want to make a sharp point on the back end of the cushions. Make a gradual curve to match the inside back of the chair (Figure 15-6). If the arms have roundness where the cushion begins to T, draw this slight roundness on your diagram (Figure 15-7). *Tip!* Use a yardstick to measure the back to front measurements and all other flat surfaces. A yardstick is rigid and easier to use than a tape measure, and more accurate when measuring flat areas. Only use the flexible tape measure when measuring areas such as the distance between inside arms, over rounded areas, and curves. The measurements you have now on your drawing are the finished sizes. You will need to add 1/2″ seam allowance on all sides. If the finished measurement of the cushion from front to back is 22″, cut the fabric 23″. This will allow a 1/2″ in the back and a 1/2″ in the front for seam allowances. When all the seam allowances have been accounted for, transfer the measurements to the fabric.

If you are working with a patterned fabric or stripe, you will need to determine the center of the pattern or stripe. If you are working with a napped fabric, remember the nap should be smooth running downwards and smooth from back to front. Determine where the center of the pattern will be on the center of the cushion top. *Tip!* If you have a back cushion that will sit on top of the seat cushion you will need to measure from the front of the back cushion to the front of the seat cushion to get a proper measurement for center (Figures 15-8 & 9). When the pattern is determined for the center of the seat cushion, measure forward to find the front edge of the cushion. Find this area on the fabric and strike a chalk line from selvage to selvage. The pattern should be the same on both sides of the fabric unless you are working with a drop matched pattern. If you have a T shaped cushion, you will most likely be working from the pattern in the center of your fabric (Figures 15-10 & 11). Make a centerline on the fabric in the center of your pattern from the front to the back. The centerline that you have marked should be the same center throughout the chair. When transferring the measurements to the fabric, work from this centerline outwards. If your cushion is to be cut at 30″ from side to side, measure 15″ outwards from the center on each side. Use the first cushion top as a pattern to cut out the other cushion top. Cut out the two faces and place them on the deck for safekeeping (Figures 15-12 & 13).

You will cut the front boxing for the cushion next. If you are working with a patterned or striped fabric the boxing must match the pattern or stripe (Figures 15-14 & 15). To match a stripe, simply measure from the center of the centered stripe outwards. If your cushion is T shaped you will most likely need two pieces of boxing. The front piece should match and will be seamed along the sides of the cushion. Since the fabric is only 54″ wide, you will need more than one 54″ width of fabric

Figure 15-16

Figure 15-17

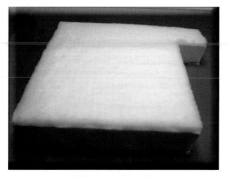

Figure 15-18

Figure 15-19

to complete the boxing. You must have seams in the boxing unless the fabric is **railroaded** (See Measuring). Avoid having seams showing on the front of the boxing. *Tip!* To match the boxing to the face of a patterned cushion, place one cut cushion top on the roll of fabric making sure to match up the patterns. Chalk a line on the cushion's front edge (Figure 15-16). Remove the cushion top and measure 1″ upwards from this chalk line. Extend this line from selvage to selvage. This is the top cut line of the boxing. Measure downwards from this line the thickness of the cut size of the boxing (Figure 15-17). If the foam you are using is 4″ thick, cut the boxing 4-1/2″. This will allow for a 1/2″ seam allowances on the top and the bottom. The finished size of the boxing will be 3-1/2″ thick. The boxing should always be narrower than the fillings. The boxing should be approximately 1/2″–1″ narrower than the fillings. This helps the cushion from shifting and rolling. *Tip!* If you are cutting new foam, lay your cut cushion top on the foam and trace around the edges. Cut the foam to this size. Since the cushion top has 1/2″ seam allowances all the way around, the foam will be cut to the perfect size. By cutting the foam larger than the cushion, it will help the finished cushion from shifting and rolling.

Tip! Polyester batting should be glued on the faces or wrapped around the two faces and the edges. This makes the cushion look fuller by adding a slight crown to the cushion tops (Figure 15-18). The batting also adds to the comfort of the cushion and cuts down on the friction between the two surfaces. Dacron batting can be added to the cushion with the use of a hand stapler (Figures 15-19 & 20). *Tip!* If you are cutting new foam for a T shaped cushion, cut approximately 1/2″ into the inside corners of the foam. This will help the foam flex in the T area and will make filling the cushion much easier. You can use an electric carving knife to cut the foam. Hold the knife perpendicular to the foam when cutting (Figure 15-21).

The zipper fabric should be cut approximately 8″ longer than the back width of the cushion. There will be approximately 4″ extra zipper fabric on each side of the cushion. This will help in filling the cushion later. Patterns do not have to match the zippers or side boxing because they will not be seen. Matching the stripes on the zipper always looks more professional (Figure 15-22). You will probably be the only one who knows the zipper stripe matches until you show off your project to all of your friends and family. Cut the zipper fabric 1-1/2″ taller than the CUT size of the boxing. If the finished size of the boxing is cut at 4-1/2″, cut the zipper fabric 6″. To make the zipper, fold the fabric face to face and sew 3/4″ in from the fold with a long basting stitch with the sewing machine (Figure 15-23). After this is sewn, cut the fabric in the center of the fold. **Do not remove the stitches yet!**

Figure 15-20

Figure 15-21

Figure 15-22

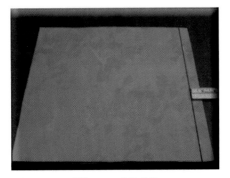

Figure 15-23

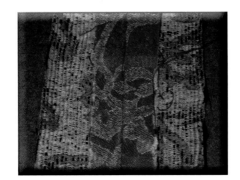

Figure 15-24

Figure 15-25

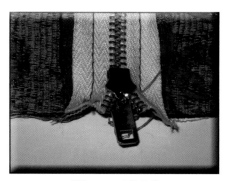

Figure 15-26

Figure 15-27

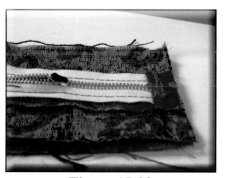

Figure 15-28

Figure 15-29

Place the fabric face down and fold over the two 3/4″ pieces of fabric. You may steam or iron the two pieces to help them lay flat (Figure 15-24). Place the cut zipper track on the sew line and center the teeth of the zipper. **Do not pull the zipper apart yet!** Most zippers will have small arrows printed on one side of the zipper tape. Sew the zipper with the arrows facing upward. The arrows indicate the direction in which the zipper will be closed (Figure 15-25). With your welt foot or zipper foot on the sewing machine, stitch along each side of the zipper tape. Keep the stitches almost to the edges of the tape. If you place the edge of the welt foot along the edge of the teeth when sewing, it should be the proper area to sew the tape. Leave enough space for the zipper pull to traverse along the teeth of the zipper. **Do not cut the stitches yet!** It is now time to install the zipper pull. With the zipper still together, place the small end of the zipper pull facing the points of the arrows. With the closing tab of the zipper pull facing outwards and towards the fabric, push the end of the zipper pull onto the zipper. Push the zipper pull as far inward as you can. Pull slightly on both sides of the zipper chain at the same time. The zipper chain should open slightly now. Slide the zipper pull approximately 3/4 of the way up the zipper track using your index finger (Figure 15-26). Sew the **closed** end of the zipper to one of the two smaller pieces of side boxing. When sewing the two pieces together, add a small piece of folded fabric over the teeth of the zipper (Figure 15-27). The folded piece of fabric makes the seam over the zipper teeth much stronger and holds the end of the zipper together (Figure 15-28). *Tip!* Walk the needle of the sewing machine over the teeth of the zipper. You can easily break the sewing machine needle when sewing over the teeth of the zipper. **Do not cut the stitches yet!**

Use a welt foot or a zipper foot when sewing the welt cord. With all the pieces of welt cord cut and neatly stacked to avoid flip flopping, place all of the pieces on your lap while seated at the sewing machine. Take the first piece of welt cord from your lap starting from the left side. Place it face up and horizontally on the sewing table in front of you. Take the second piece of welt cord from your lap, again from the left side. You want to keep all of the welt cords running in the same direction. *Tip!* If you flip-flop a velvet fabric the color of the welt cord will change drastically from one piece to another. Place the second piece of welt on top of the first piece of welt that is on your sewing table. Place this second piece of welt fabric vertically on the right hand side of the first piece of welt fabric and face-to-face. This should form a 90° angle. Leave approximately 3/4″ of fabric extending over each end (Figure 15-29). Sew the two pieces together starting at the top left corner and sewing across the welt to the bottom right corner (Figure 15-30). Repeat this step until you have sewn all the pieces together to form one long piece (Figure 15-31). Think of the number 7 when sewing the welt cords together. This is the shape before sewing. *Tip!* By leaving the extra 3/4″ on each end of the welt when sewing, you will immediately

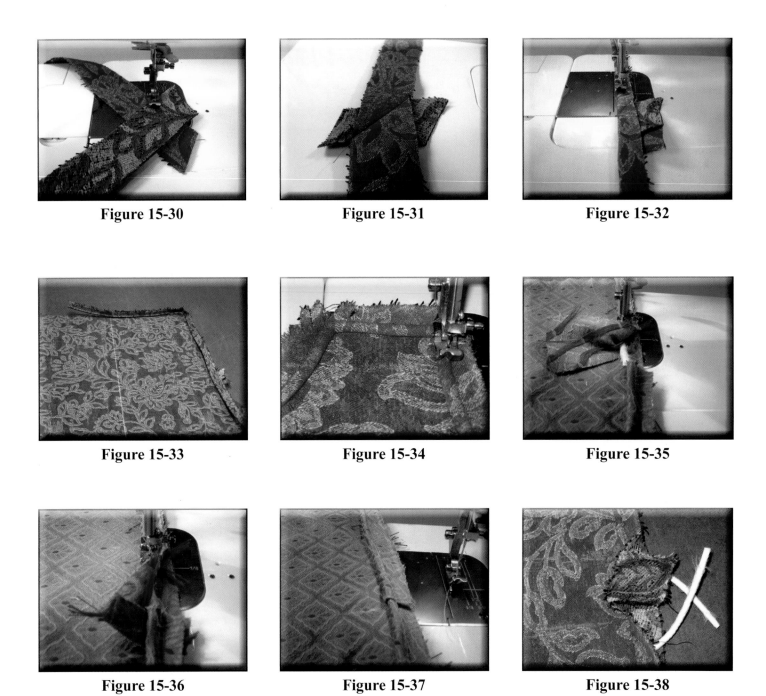

Figure 15-30

Figure 15-31

Figure 15-32

Figure 15-33

Figure 15-34

Figure 15-35

Figure 15-36

Figure 15-37

Figure 15-38

Figure 15-39

Figure 15-40

Figure 15-41

Figure 15-42

see where there is a seam. You will not have to hunt for the seams later (Figure 15-32). Do not cut off the extra fabric from the seams. You will cut off the extra when you sew the welt onto the fabric or staple it to the chair.

Sew the welt cord onto each face of the cushion. Make sure not to have any seams on the front edges of the cushions. Always start sewing the welt cord by leaving approximately 3″ of welt cord not sewn (Figure 15-33). You will be finishing the end of the welt later. As you sew the welt cord and approach a corner, stop and make small cuts into the tail of the welt cord (Figure 15-34). *Tip!* Make sure one of the cuts is exactly on the corner. This will help the welt cord turn the corner. Remember to keep the tail of the welt cord even with the edge of the cushion. This is your 1/2″ seam allowance. *Tip!* When you sew the welt cord to the face and you are turning the corner, keep the needle in the down position on the corner. Lift the foot of the machine, pivot the cushion top and then give the welt cord a little bend or crack. This helps the welt cord pivot around the corner. Lower the foot on the machine and continue sewing the welt cord until there is approximately 3″ remaining. Cut the welt cord approximately 3″ longer than the end of the first piece. Open up the seams on the two pieces of welt cord and lay the two pieces of rope next to each other and cut them so that they butt up to one another (Figure 15-35). Overlap one of the welt fabrics and turn the raw edge under (Figure 15-36). Continue sewing to finish the welt (Figure 15-37). *Tip!* If the fabric is too thick to overlap, perform all the other steps but you will sew the two pieces of welt cord together. To do this, pinch the two welts together face to face. Walk your fingers down the welt cords until you reach the point where the two pieces will meet on the face of the cushion. Mark this spot and sew the two pieces of fabric together on the sewing machine (Figure 15-38). Trim the excess fabric and finish by folding the seam allowances back and sewing the remainder of welt cord to the face of the cushion (Figures 15-39 through 41).

You will now sew the boxing to the faces of the cushion. With the welt cords sewn into place, line up the long center piece of boxing to the cushion face. Match up the pattern or stripe and pin the two pieces of fabric together (Figure 15-42). Stretch the boxing in each direction to the corners and pin into place. Work the boxing around the corners to determine where the second pieces of boxing will be sewn to the center piece on the sides. Place the zipper on the back of the cushion and match if striped. Pin the zipper into place. Sew the side boxing that has the **closed** side of the zipper track to the front boxing. Do not sew the open side of the zipper to the boxing yet (Figure 15-43). Start sewing the boxing on the front of the cushion if you have a pattern fabric. Be sure to match the pattern. Continue sewing until you reach the open-end of the zipper. Stop sewing the boxing approximately 4" to 6" short of the

Figure 15-43

Figure 15-44

Figure 15-45

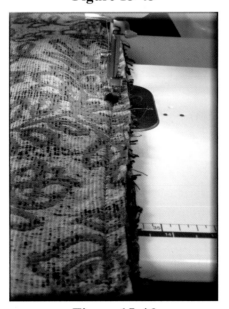

Figure 15-46

open end of the zipper (Figure 15-44). If you have sewn the boxing to this point with the cushion right side up, you will continue sewing the remainder of the boxing upside down. You will basically turn the cushion over and sew on the other side. Sew one time with the welt side up and the other time with the welt side down (Figure 15-45). If your fabric is plain and does not need to match, start sewing at the open side of the zipper. Keep the edges of the boxing even with the edge of the cushion and clip the boxing just before you turn a corner, just like you did when you sewed the welt to the faces (Figure 15-46). Now finish sewing the open end of the zipper. Cut the side boxing approximately 4″ longer than the end of the zipper. Sew the end of the boxing to the end of the zipper (Figure 15-47). Place a small piece of folded fabric over the teeth of the zipper when you sew over this area. Remember to walk the needle over the zipper by hand, making sure not to break the needle. With the remainder of fabric, fold the zippered part of the fabric over the extra boxing. The zipper should be on the outside, and the extra boxing will be on the inside facing the cushion. This folded area will be the pocket for the zipper (Figure 15-48). By sewing a pocket, the zipper pull will be hidden and will not rub the inside arm area. This rubbing can wear out the fabric quickly. The other side of the cushion will now be sewn to the boxing. Clip the corners to indicate where to line up the corners. To clip the corners, pinch the two sides of the boxing together. Looking downwards, line up the corner and make a very small clip in the fabric (Figures 15-49 & 50). With square corners you can fold each side over and you should have the same amount of fabric on both sides. *Tip!* Pin the corners of the boxing you just marked together to the other side of the cushion face. Slightly pull the boxing to stretch the other side of the fabric (Figure 15-51). If there is a small amount of extra fabric remaining on the boxing to be sewn, pin the remaining boxing and sew it to the other side of the cushion. When you are done sewing, clip and remove the basting stitch from the zipper track and turn the cushion right side out. If the corners are bulky, clip them before turning the cover right side out (Figure 15-52).

Before inserting the fillings into the cushion cover, determine if the old foam padding will be used or new foam padding will be used. If the old foam has lost its resiliency and does not spring back into shape, it is time to replace it. After the foam is cut to size you can spray glue polyester batting onto each face by gluing both surfaces. Wait a short amount of time before applying the two surfaces together. You can also use Dacron wrap and hand sew, or staple this padding into place. You can cover the sides of the foam as well as each face.

To fill the cushion cover, place the cover on your table with the zipper facing you. Fold the foam cushion in half and hold it together with one hand. With your other hand open the back of the cushion. Place the foam in the cushion as far forward as possible. Squeeze the sides

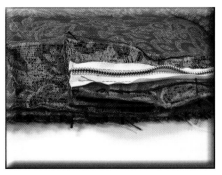

Figure 15-47

Figure 15-48

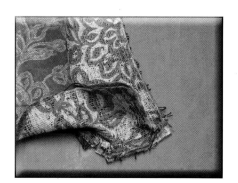

Figure 15-49

Figure 15-50

Figure 15-51

Figure 15-52

Figure 15-53

Figure 15-54

Figure 15-55

of the foam while pushing the foam towards the front of the cushion. Yes, this is going to be tough. Move the foam to the corners by pushing the foam forward on the sides and from the center of the front to the corners. *Tip!* After the foam is worked into all of the corners make sure all of the tails of the welt cords are against the sides of the foam and not the top of the foam. This will keep the welt cord standing up straight and give the cushion a crisp look. Keep the cushion as flat as possible when filling the foam and working the tails of the welt cord into position. A small amount of loose Dacron or polyester batting can be inserted into the corners to help fill them out if needed. To close the zipper, push the foam forward while holding the cushion cover. Make sure the tails of the welt cords are on the side of the foam again. Pull the zipper tab a few inches and repeat this step until the zipper is closed. Be careful not to get the batting caught in the zipper. The zipper pull should now be hidden in the pocket of the cushion. Place the finished cushion into the chair, step back and say, "Wow, I did it!" (Figures 15-53 through 55)

Chapter 16 | Footstool

Figure 16-1

Figure 16-2

Figure 16-3

If you are making a foot stool to match your chair, the fabric pattern should also match the chair. The pattern or stripe that was used as center on the chair should also be used as the center on the foot stool (Figure 16-1). Measure the frame and add a 1/2″ seam allowance to all sides. The boxing should match the top of the foot stool (Figure 16-2). The foot stool top should be sewn like a cushion but without the bottom and zipper (see Cushion Making). Be sure to add enough fabric on the bottom of the boxing for pulling and stapling. Sew a welt cord to the face of the stool top (Figures 16-3 through 16-6). If the fabric you are using is not railroaded, the boxing fabric will have to be seamed. The seaming should be done on the corners. Stop sewing the boxing a few inches from the corners. Use a square to help mark the proper area to cut the boxing. Place the square on the edge of the stool top. The stool top already has 1/2″ seam allowances (Figures 16-7 & 8). Sew the two pieces of boxing together. The seam should line up on the corner (Figure 16-9). Clip the bulk from the corners when the boxing has been sewn (Figure 16-10). Place the sewn fabric on the foot stool and pull the boxing over the sides and loose tack it to the bottom of the frame (Figure 16-11). The tail of the welt cord should be on the side of the stool and not the top. This will insure a crisp look to the welt cord as opposed to laying flat. Use a yardstick to help determine the proper height of the boxing (Figure 16-12). *Tip!* A piece of cardboard tack strip can be used as a gauge to insure the proper height of the boxing all the way around the stool (Figure 16-13). When the boxing has been loose tacked at the proper height, remove the tacks from the center areas and replace with staples. Start at the centers and work your way to the legs (Figure 16-14). Remember to stop stapling the boxing a few inches from each leg. To cut the fabric around the legs, start cutting from the center of the leg up to where the leg meets the frame on the inside corners (Figure 16-15). Cut off the bulk from this cut and turn the raw edges under and staple over the top of the leg (Figures 16-16 & 17). A base welt trim will be added to cover these staples next. Start stapling the base welt trim leaving a few inches not stapled because it will make it easier to finish the ends later. The tail of the welt will be notched out around the leg area (Figure 16-18). Hot glue should be added where the fabric is notched out to keep it secure to the frame (Figure 16-19). Finish the ends of the welt cord by folding one end of the fabric over the other and stapling the end into place (Figures 16-20 & 21). Cambric is added to the bottom to give it a finished look. Cut

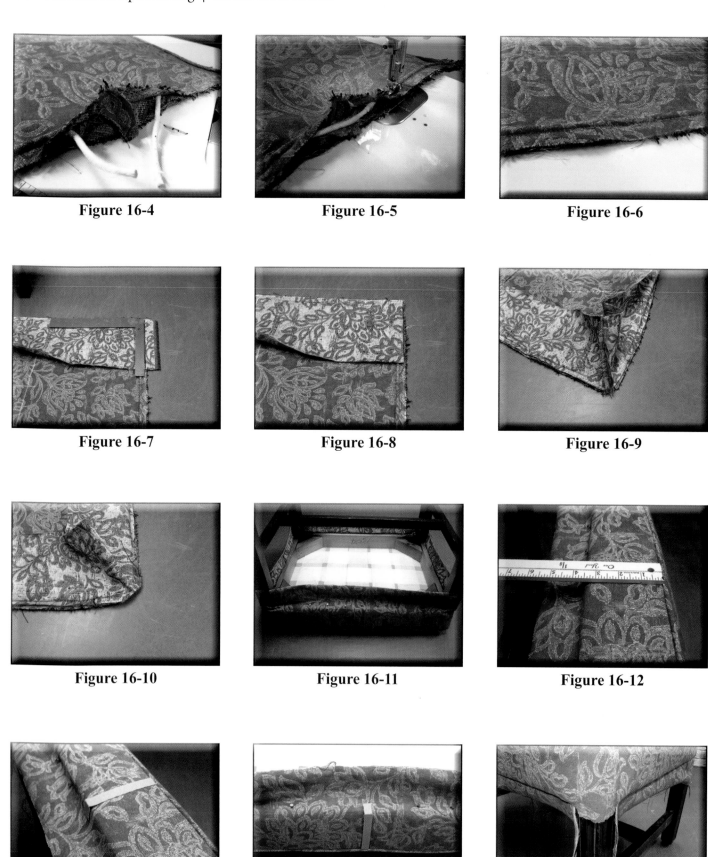

Figure 16-4

Figure 16-5

Figure 16-6

Figure 16-7

Figure 16-8

Figure 16-9

Figure 16-10

Figure 16-11

Figure 16-12

Figure 16-13

Figure 16-14

Figure 16-15

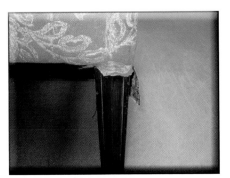

Figure 16-16

Figure 16-17

Figure 16-18

Figure 16-19

Figure 16-20

Figure 16-21

Figure 16-22

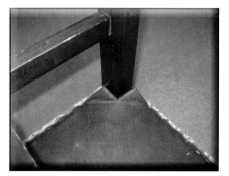

Figure 16-23

Figure 16-24

the cambric a little larger than the stool and fold the edges under and staple the cambric into place stopping short of the corners. Fold back the edges to form a point (Figure 16-22). Cut the cambric from this point to the inside corner of the leg. Fold the raw edges under and staple into place (Figures 16-23 through 24).

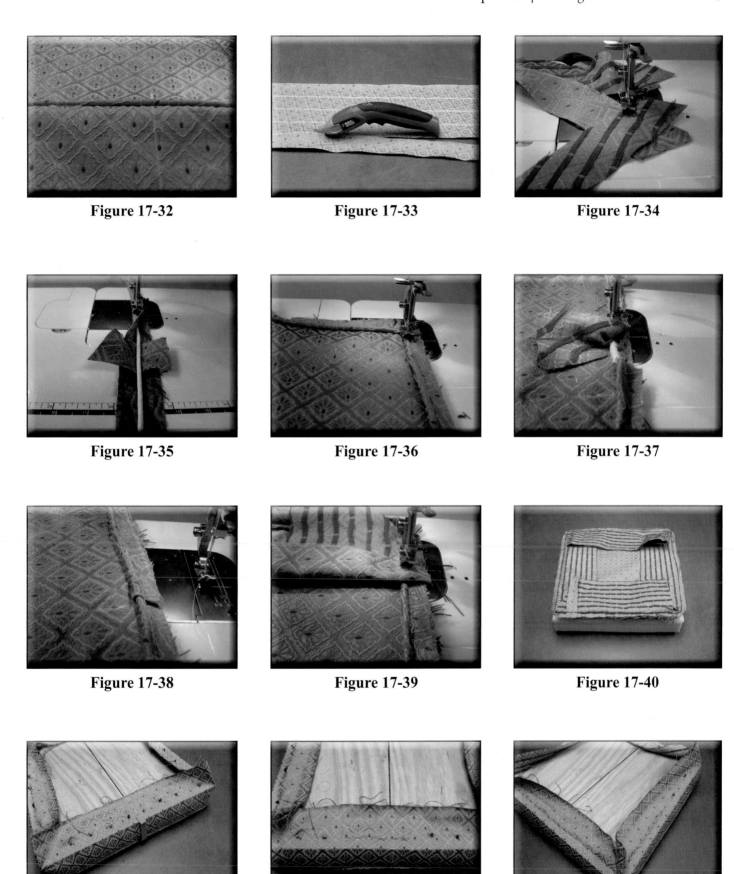

Figure 17-32

Figure 17-33

Figure 17-34

Figure 17-35

Figure 17-36

Figure 17-37

Figure 17-38

Figure 17-39

Figure 17-40

Figure 17-41

Figure 17-42

Figure 17-43

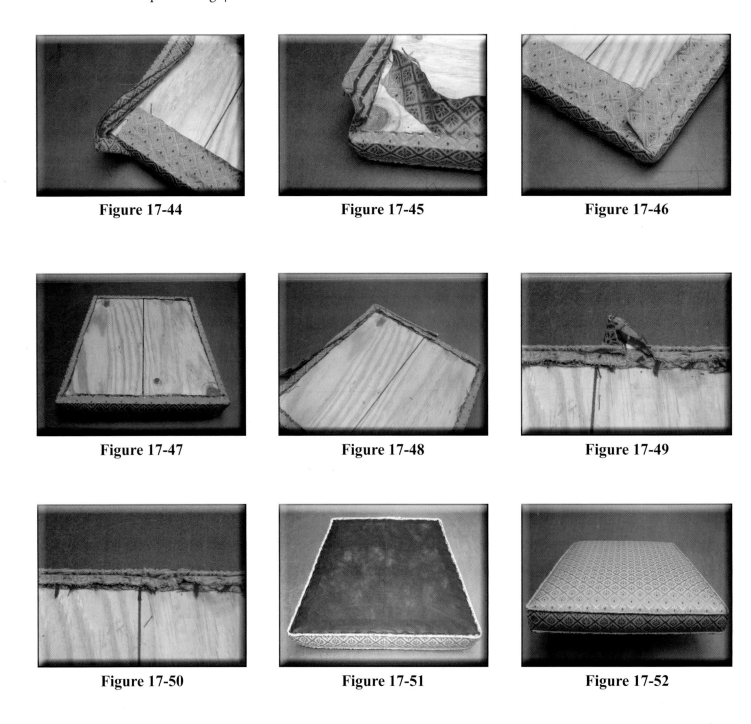

Figure 17-44

Figure 17-45

Figure 17-46

Figure 17-47

Figure 17-48

Figure 17-49

Figure 17-50

Figure 17-51

Figure 17-52

Figure 17-53

Chapter 18 | Zippered Pillow Making

Figure 18-1

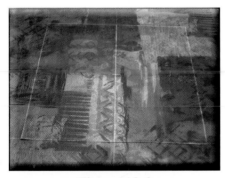

Figure 18-2

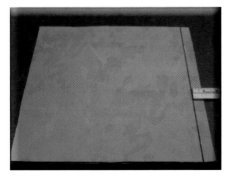

Figure 18-3

Before you begin to make your pillow, please read "Cutting Cushions and Pillows with a Crown".

To begin, select the fabric to be used. If the fabric is patterned or striped, make sure to chalk a centerline. If you are using a napped fabric, make sure that the nap is running smoothly from the top to the bottom on both faces.

Determine the finished size of the pillow. The finished size will be measured from pleat to pleat. Add 2″ to the finished size of the pillow. This will be the cut size of the two faces. If you want your pillow to be 14″ finished, cut the fabric 16″. If a pattern such as a floral bouquet is to be used, all measurements will be taken from the center of the pattern (Figure 18-1). From the centerline, measure outwards in both directions 1/2 of the cut size of the pillow. Do this on the top and the bottom of the pattern. Strike a chalk line to connect these marks on both sides of the pattern. These lines are your side-to-side measurements. To determine where to mark the top and bottom of the pillow, start measuring from the center of the pattern again. This time you will measure upwards and downwards, 1/2 of the cut size. Place a square on the edges to make sure the edges of the pillow are square and adjust the lines if needed. When working with a striped fabric, measure from the center of the stripe outwards, just like working with a pattern. When one of the up and down lines is made, chalk the side-to-side lines using a square. Place one edge of the square on one of the up and down lines and chalk a line using the other side of the square. This will give you a square edge to work from. Cut this pillow face and use it as a pattern to cut the second face. Make sure the faces are square and exactly the same size (Figure 18-2).

Place the two pieces of fabric you just cut face-to-face. Make sure the patterns are running in the proper direction. Measure up from the bottom 3/4″ and sew them together using a long basting stitch (Figures 18-3 & 4). A basting stitch is a long stitch that can be easily removed later. Place the two faces downwards. You should see the two 3/4″ pieces facing you. You can steam or iron the two pieces to lay flat. Place the zipper chain over these two pieces and sew on the edges of

85

Figure 18-4

Figure 18-5

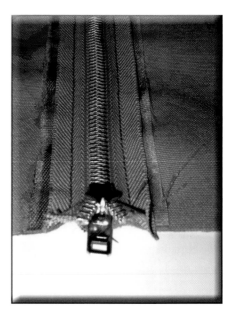

Figure 18-6

Figure 18-7

Figure 18-8

Figure 18-9

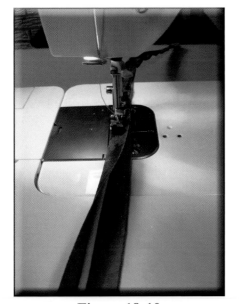

Figure 18-10

Figure 18-11

the tape (Figure 18-5). **Do not** separate the zipper chain at this time or put the zipper pull on. You can use your welt foot or zipper foot to sew the zipper in place. In most cases, you can keep the edge of the welt foot against the edge of the teeth and sew down each side of the zipper tape. Keep the stitches close to the outside edge of the zipper tape. The zipper pull will have to traverse. If the stitches are too close to the teeth, the zipper pull will not be able to slide from side-to-side. You should see small arrows printed on the zipper tape. These arrows indicate which way the zipper pull will close. Make sure you can see the arrows when you are sewing the zipper in place. Now it is time to install the zipper pull. With the zipper still together, place the small end of the zipper pull facing the points of the arrows. With the closing tab of the zipper pull facing outwards and towards the fabric, push the end of the zipper pull onto the zipper. Push the zipper pull as far inward as you can. Pull slightly on both sides of the zipper chain at the same time. The zipper chain should open slightly now. Slide the zipper pull approximately 3/4 of the way up the zipper using your index finger. **Do not cut the basting stitch yet!** (Figure 18-6)

The pleats will now be sewn into the top corners on both faces. Fold one of the top corners face to face bringing the two cut sides together to form a point. Measure inward and along the cut side of the fabric. Sew this corner 1″ inward from the point of the fabric (Figure 18-7). Trim the excess leaving 1/2″ from the sew line (Figure 18-8). Repeat this step on the other top corners. When the pillow is completed, you will have a 1/2″ pleat. The other 1/2″ of this 1″ pleat you have sewn will be taken up by the seam allowance of the welt cord.

Cut a piece of fabric for the welt cord. This will be 1-1/2″ wide, cut on the bias, and contain no seams if possible (Figure 18-9). To make welt cord, use your welt foot or zipper foot. Place the cord into the center of the fabric. Roll the two edges of the fabric together around the cord. Sew next to the cord and keep the two edges of the fabric even. This will be your 1/2″ seam allowance (Figure 18-10), from the sew line to the edge of the fabric. The most common size of welt cord is 5/32″. After the welt cord is sewn, begin to sew it onto one of the faces. The pillow will have only one welt cord. This style is called knife edged (Figure 18-11). When a welt cord is applied on both sides of the boxing like a cushion, this style is called a boxed edge. Start sewing the welt cord in the center of the zipper track and continue sewing until you are a few inches short of the first sewn pleated corner. Make a few cuts into the tail of the welt cord. Start the cuts just before the sewn pleated corner. Make sure one of the cuts is on the corner. This will help the welt cord turn the corner. Make sure to keep the tail of the welt cord even with the edge of the pillow when sewing. *Tip!* When you are sewing the welt cord to the face of the fabric and get to a corner, raise the foot up and

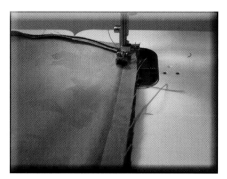

Figure 18-12

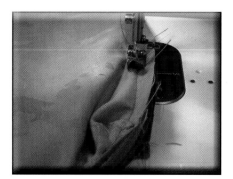

Figure 18-13

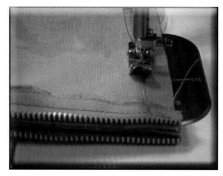

Figure 18-14

Figure 18-15

keep the needle of the sewing machine in the down position when you want to turn the corner. Pivot the fabric towards you and give the welt cord a little kink, or crack. This will help bend the welt cord to make a square corner. Drop the foot down and continue sewing the welt cord and end on the other center of the zipper track. Now the two faces will be sewn together.

Tip! When the welt is sewn onto the face it can sometimes cause a little shrinkage. This side can sometimes be smaller than the side that does not have the welt sewn onto it. To make sewing the pillow together easier, sew with the welt side on the top. The fabric without the welt cord will be on the bottom. This will help you pull the welted side of the fabric when sewing. It is easier to pull the welted side if it is on the topside, as opposed to the bottom side. Start sewing on the open side of the zipper. Pinch the zipper so that the zipper teeth from both sides of the zipper track are on top on one another (Figure 18-12). When sewing the faces together and the needle in the down position, pull the welt slightly when sewing. Check to see if the seams on the corners will line up properly. Adjust by not pulling the welt, or pulling the welt cord even more. You can also pin the corners at the seams to make this sewing process easier if needed (Figures 18-13 & 14). After the pillow has been sewn once, I recommend re-sewing the welted seam again to tighten the sew line. Try to sew closer to the welt cord. After the welted seam has been sewn a second time, trim off 1/2 of the tail of the welt cord. This will help the welt cord stand straighter and look crisper when the pillow is filled. Now it's time to sew the bottom pleats at the zipper (Figure 18-15).

Start the bottom pleats by pinching the fabric on each side of the welt cord. Pull slightly on both sides. The welt cord should be centered on top of the zipper track. If there is a lot of bulk over the zipper, hammer the area down with your tack hammer (Figure 18-16). Sew across the zipper with a small piece of fabric folded over the teeth. Sew back and forth and 1″ inward from the end (Figure 18-17). Be careful not to break your sewing machine needle. Walk the needle over the teeth by hand. Cut off the bulk and repeat this step on the other side of the zipper (Figure 18-18). Now it is time to cut the basting stitch out of the zipper track (Figure 18-19). Turn the pillow right side out (Figures 18-20 & 21).

When filling the pillow it is best to use a high-quality pillow core and not scraps of cotton or polyester. When choosing a pillow core, always select a larger size to install into your pillow (this will help to fill out and keep the shape of the pillow). If your pillow finishes at 14″ from pleat to pleat, install a 16″ pillow core. To ensure the corners are full looking, add a small amount of loose Dacron or polyester batting to all four corners (Figures 18-22 & 23).

Figure 18-16

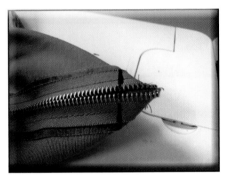

Figure 18-17

Figure 18-18

Figure 18-19

Figure 18-20

Figure 18-21

Figure 18-22

Figure 18-23

Chapter 19 | Commonly Used Hand Tools

Safety should always be your first priority when working with any tool. Always use extreme caution and remember to wear eye protection.

When it comes to tools, upholstering is no different than any other trade. You must have the correct tool to perform the job properly. Quality tools are an investment that will last a lifetime. In my opinion, the finest quality hand tools for the upholstering industry are made by C. S. Osborne & Co. A complete list of these quality hand tools can be found on the following pages. Some tools used in the upholstering trade can be very costly and will seldom be used by the do-it-yourselfer. I have listed below the tools that are used on a daily basis.

These quality hand tools can be purchased through my website at www.GrindstonePublishing.com. Tools are normally shipped the next day. Specialized hand tool orders are accepted, and will usually be shipped within a few days.

 #120 1/2 Staple knocker

 #33 Magnetic tack hammer

 #255 Webbing stretcher

 #K-5 Straight round point needles

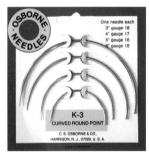 #K-3 Curved round point needles

 #306 ½ 10″ Flat regulator

C.S. OSBORNE & CO. HARRISON, NJ 07029 - U.S.A.

UPHOLSTERY TOOLS

BRONZE MAGNETIC HAMMER
(with solid head)

Osborne No. 33

Solid head bronze. Steel tipped, one end for permanent alnico magnet the other for hammering.

Length of head (inches)	Weight of head (oz)	Magnetic face(inches)	Large face (inches)	Weight ea (oz)
5 1/2	7	1/4	7/16	11

BARREL SHAPED HICKORY MALLET

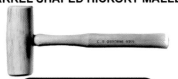

Osborne No. 89-1/2

Made of second growth hickory, a carefull finished, well balanced. Lacquered.

Size No.	Diameter of face (inches)	Diameter of head (inches)	Weight ea (oz)
2 1/2	2 3/8	5 1/2	16
3	2 1/4	5 1/2	12
3 1/2	2	5 1/4	12
4	1 3/4	5	8

STRIPPING HAMMER

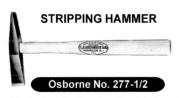

Osborne No. 277-1/2

Forged tools steel double edged for stripping off old fabrics. Length of head is 5 inches. Width of bits is 13/16 inches. Weighs 20 oz.

MAGNETIC HAMMER

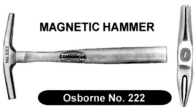

Osborne No. 222

Similar as above but heavier and longer. Also with perfect balance. Length of head 5-1/2". Magnetic face 5/16". Large face 1/2"

UPHOLSTERY REGULATORS

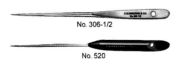

No. 306-1/2

No. 520

Osborne No. 306-1/2

With eye. 6", 8", 10" and 12" available in light, heavy and extra light. Also available with plastic handle.

OSBORNE FANCY NAIL HAMMER
(with nylon tip)

Osborne No. 36

Similar our popular No. 33 Bronze Magnetic Hammer, but the large face is fitted with a nylon tip. This prevents damage to ornamental nails.

Length of head (inches)	Weight of head (oz)	Magnetic face(inches)	Large face (inches)	Weight ea (oz)
5 1/2	6	1/4	7/16	11

HOME UPHOLSTERY REPAIR KIT

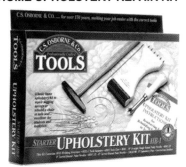

Osborne No. HB1

Includes Easy to Follow Instruction book. Also available B4, B7 & B11 Upholstery Kits.

TUCKING TOOL

Osborne No. 747

For tucking headlining and upholstery around windows and above doors and other hard to reach places. A sturdy tough tool with a slightly curved blade that has finishes edges around corners. Available also with flexible blade **Osborne No. 746.**

SCRATCH AWL

Osborne No. 4

Made in four sizes. Best quality blades with rugged amber translucent plastic handles. Blades length available in: 2-1/2", 3-1/2", 4-1/2" and 5-1/2".

STAPLE LIFTER

Osborne No. 1066

Polished and forged steel blade. Hardwood handle. A European favorite

STAPLE LIFTER

Osborne No. 120 1/2

The correct angle for removing staples of any size, from the smallest to the long leg staples and shreded material. Manufactured from top grade steel. Electronically hardened working ends. Easy to grip plastic handle. Very popular.

TACK CLAW

Osborne No. 202

A quality drop-forged tack claw. Pointed ends are hardened and tempered to prevent breakage. Also available with wooden handle Osborne No. 201.

TACK AND STAPLE REMOVER

Osborne No. 121

Made of forged steel with wooden handle.

STAPLE REMOVER

Osborne No. 124

Forged from 4140 alloy tempered steel. Carefully hardened for lasting use. Wooden handle.

RIPPING TOOL

Osborne No. 402

A beautifully finished tool with a new type of translucent amber handle designed to fit the hand with perfect balance. Forged, highly polished steel blade with chisel edge. Shouldered tang to prevent driving into handle. Length 8-3/4", width of blade 1/2".

BAZOOKA

Osborne No. 302

Save time and money with this high performance jet stream. Fill cushions, pillows, mattresses, and much more, the easy way. Instructions enclosed. Made of aluminum. Overall 28".

SEAM STRETCHER

Osborne No. 267

Also made of light weight aluminum. Simple toggle clamp construction. Easy to operate. Length expaxion range is from 12" to 3". Rigid when in use. No springs or chains. Larger capacity. Easy to follow instructions in each package. Points easily replace with points of No. 190 3" Upholstery Pins.

We carry the mot complete line of needles. Write for free catalogue of tools and needles.

C.S. OSBORNE & CO. HARRISON, NJ 07029 - U.S.A.

UPHOLSTERY TOOLS

ZIPPER STOPS PLIERS

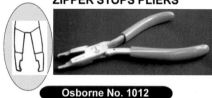

Osborne No. 1012

Made of high quality steel. Vinyl handles for easy gripping. Open spring designed to install any kind of stops on zippers. Patent pending.

OSBORNE U-CUT FOAM RUBBER SLICER (cuts slabs horizontally)

Osborne No. 410

U-cut will cut from a minimum of 1/4" to a maximum thickness of 9". Material of up to 36" in width and unlimited length can be processed. You can glue salvageable large material and use every piece of it.

ALUMINUM RULERS
(inches and metric)

Osborne No. 161

This 5 ft. rule is made of anodized aluminum. It is 1-1/2" wide and is tempered to stay straight. One side shows graduations in inches along both edges with measurements also from center of rule. When turned over, the opposite side of the rule has graduations in millimeters and centimeters along one side.

Osborne No. 60SE

One of the finest measuring rules on the market. Marking on one side only. Heavy wide aluminum. Hole on one end for hanging.

REVOLVING PUNCH

Osborne No. 155

The best ever made. Forged steel highly polished. 6 cutting tubes turned from special carbon tool steel.

Osborne No. 223

Quality pressed frame with drive punches.

T-PINS

Osborne No. 189

Length 20: 1-1/4", 24: 1-1/2, 28: 1-3/4" $ 32: 2".

UPHOLSTERY PINS

Osborne No. 190

Length 3", 3-1/2" and 4". All 16 gauge.

COLOR GLASS HEAD PINS

No. 181=1-1/2" and No. 178 = 2" are available.

COLOR UPHOLSTERY PINS

Osborne No. 193

Length 2-1/8. Gauge 17. Red, blue, white, yellow and green. Packed 100 per box.

TUFTING NEEDLE "TIMESAVER"

Osborne No. 417

* No need to turn fabric to be tufted.
* Every tufting done from above.
* Avoids soiling which comes with repeated handling.
* Always a straight seam.
* Less effort. Clasps automatically ejected.
* Fewer stitches.
* Tufts buttons easily.
* Overall time saving.
    Use with Osborne No. 418 Clasps

ROUND POINT NEEDLES

K-3   K-4   K-7

Osborne No. K-3

It is composed of four curved round point needles 3", 4", 5" and 6".

Osborne No. K-4

Same as above but with diamond point needles.

Osborne No. K-7

Composed on four curved round point needles extra light needles 2-1/", 3", 3-1/2" and 4" per card.

STRAIGHT POINT NEEDLES

Osborne No. K-5

Four to a card. Sizes 6", 8" 10" and 12". Each card printed in attractive yellow and blue and is cellophane covered to protect against dust.

Osborne No. K-6

Composed of 1 each of double end round point needles sizes: 10", 12" and 14".

GROMMET INSERTING DIE
(die forged steel)

Osborne No. 216

Sets plain rim washers and grommets. Sizes 00 to 5 drop forged, size 6 malleable casting. Properly machined and hardened. For best results use only Osborne grommets and washers.

| Sizes: | 00 | 0 | 1 | 2 | 3 | 4 | 5 | 6 |

Use our No. 217 grommet inserting die to set No. G2 brass rolled rim grommets and spur washers. Nickel plated brass grommets also available.

BRASS PLAIN RIM GROMMETS AND PLAIN WASHERS.

Osborne No. G1

For best results in setting No. G1 grommets and washers use an Osborne No. 500 hole punch and an Osborne No. 216 setting die with corresponding sizes.

Size No.	00	0	1	2	3	4	5	6
Diameter of hole when set (inches)	3/16	1/4	9/32	3/8	7/16	1/2	5/8	13/16

Biggest size 1-1/2" spur grommets brass & nickel #10

GROMMET HOLE CUTTER

Osborne No. 500

Drop forged, tempered and polished edge. Inside tapered for easy clearance. Use with corresponding grommets and setting dies.

Hole Cutter	00	0	1	2	3	4	5	6	7	8
Hole Size	3/16	1/4	9/32	3/8	7/16	1/2	5/8	3/4	7/8	1

ARCH PUNCH

Osborne No. 149

Drop forged in one piece from the finest special carbon steel in sizes from 3/16". Larger sizes are made with our properly engineered two piece welded construction. A unique feature of the Osborne arch punch is the inside taper which permits the punching to clear easily through the barrel. Fully polished barrel and black enamel handle. Also available in millimeters with green enamel finish.

C.S. OSBORNE & CO. HARRISON, NJ 07029 - U.S.A.

QUALITY

UPHOLSTERY TOOLS

BUTTON MACHINE

Osborne No. W-1

High quality hand machine. Cuts fabric and covers buttons. Uses 2 piece dies and short cutters. It has a reinforced frame and handle. Bolts to a table for added stability. Comes complete with a nylon block for cutting covers. It produces 80 to 120 buttons per hour. Also used to set snaps, grommets and ventilators. Nylon block and dowel can be also buy separately.

BUTTON DIES & CUTTERS

Precision machined, nickel plated made of high quality steel. Cutters are heat treated and have sharp edges engineered for accurate cutting and long life.

GROMMET DIE & HOLE CUTTERS

Osborne No. WDIGRC1

Designed to fit our W-1 machine. Available in sizes 00 up to 6. Sets plain grommets and washers.

SNAPS DIES

Osborne No. WDISN41

Designed to set our # 24 line of snaps when you use our W-1 machine.

BUTTONS MOLDS

Available in most pupular sizes: 9/16", 5/8", 3/4", 7/8" 1", 1-1/8", 1-1/4" and 1-1/2" diameter when covered. Many styles of backs available. Sold by 1 or 5 gross boxes.

JOINED PIVOTS OR TWIN BUTTONS

Pivot back (female)

Pivot tack (male)

Complete pivot

Shell

When a design calls for buttons on both sides of a pillow or cushion, chair backs, etc. use our Joined Pivots. It is composed of two parts: the female part which is the single pivot back and the male part which is the pivot tack . Both come in the following sizes: 22, 24, 30, 36, 40, 45 & 60. The female half is assembled with a retaining pivot spring steel lock washer which mates with the serrated pivot tack of the male half. Although easily snapped together by hand pressure, the buttons hold tight. Length of tack available are 3/5", 1/2", 3/4" and 1". Sold by sets of 1 gross box.

HOME GROMMET KIT

SET IT YOURSELF GROMMET KIT

Osborne No. K235

A complete and inexpensive Kit. Each kit consists of a No.235 grommet die, a No. 245 cutting punch, 36 of G-1 grommets and washers, a small cutting board and complete instructions. Available in sizes 00 to 6.

SQUARE POINT KNIFE

Osborne No. 76 1/2

Trimmers' and Upholsterers' knife, white blade and pinned blade. Length of blade 3-7/8". Width of blade 5/8".

SHARP POINT KNIFE

Osborne No. 79

White handle, sharp point knife. A popular knife in the shoe and leather industries. Length of blade 3-3/4". Width of blade 3/4".

AUTO TRIMMERS & UPHOLSTERERS' COMBINATION KNIFE

Osborne No. 1020

Has a hook and pointed blade. Used for ripping seams. Cuts auto carpeting vinyl, plastic and rubber. Beechwood handlet contoured to fin hand. A handy professional tool.

MARKING CHALKS

Osborne No. 88

Our chalk is clay based and thus it is much easier to erase. Other chalks that are not clay based will leave a grease mark on cottons and other fabrics. Also works on glass vinyl that other chalks do not. Due to the shape of this chalk a sharp marking edge is maintained. Contains 12 chalks: 8 white chalks, 1 red chalk, 2 yellow chalks and 1 blue chalk.

Osborne No. 85

Same as above but all chalks are white.

SKIFE KNIVE

Osborne No. 925

For skiving leather and other materials. Increases both speed and accuracy. It is fitted with a special razor blade. Nickel plated finish. Extra blades are also available.

QUICK NAILER (for spacing fancing nails)

Osborne No. 777

Set up nails head to head at one time without damaging the furniture or your fingers and get EXACT spacing at the same time.

ANTIQUE DECORATIVE NAILS

No.	Type	Lenght of tack	Standard Package	Description
680 7/16" diameter	Oxford Hammered	1/2" 5/8" 3/4"		
681 3/8" diameter	French Natural Small	1/2" 5/8" 3/4"		
682 * 7/16" diameter	French Natural Regular	1/2" 5/8" 3/4"	1,000 nails per box or 1,000 box. packaged 100 per poly bag.	Osborne highly popular Antique nails are packed 1,000 per box or 10 self-selling poly bags with an attractive header card for rack display holding 100 nails. **Two different standard packages**
683 7/16" diameter	Daisy Ornamental	1/2" 5/8" 3/4"		
684 7/16" diameter	Overlap	1/2" 5/8" 3/4"		
685 7/16" & 5/8" diameter	Spanish	1/2"		
* Osborne No. 682, also available in nickel plated				

C.S. OSBORNE & CO.
HARRISON, NJ 07029 - U.S.A.

QUALITY

UPHOLSTERY TOOLS

CARDED GROMMET KITS

Osborne No. K234

Hang up card in an easy to use display box. Complete instructions on back of card. For Do-It-Yourself Home Repair. Kit has grommet die, punch, cutting board and grommets. Sizes zero, double zero and one, four dozen of brass grommets; sizes two, three and four have two dozen of brass grommets. Cards measure 10-1/2" x 5". 6 kits to a box. **Also available with nickel plated grommets Osborne No. K231.**

LEVER SPRING STRETCHER

Osborne No. 268

Sturdy tool used for heavy duty installations and is a safe method for installing sinuous type springs. Just set spring into rear frame clip and then pull spring into position from the front of the frame.

CLIP FOR RUBBER WEBBING

Osborne No. 239

Packed 250 or 1,250 per box.

GLUE STICKS

Osborne No. 2000

SPRING BENDER

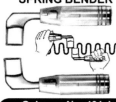

Osborne No. 401-1

Nickel plated ends are slotted to fit loops which can be bent with slight pressure or can be used to un-bend previously made bends. Also in 2".

PATTERN AND CABINET MAKERS STEEL PING DOGS.

Osborne No. 89

Square corners over legs makes easy driving.

Length (inches)								
3/4	1	1-1/4	1-1/2	2	2-1/2	2-3/4	3	3-1/2

GOOSENECK WEBBING STRETCHER

Osborne No. 253

A handy stretcher to catch the webbing close to the frame with plenty of leverage. For right or left hand. 10" overall. Width 4".

HOG RING PLIERS
(with vinyl handles)

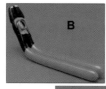

Osborne No. 1440

Nine different styles with straight or angled handles, some with opening springs, some with closing springs, others with no springs. Please specify style-grooves are the proper depth. Made of forged steel.

1440-A	Straight handles 6-3/4"	Jaws and handles are aligned
1440-B	Handles bent at 135 degree angle to jaw	
1440-C	Handles bent to reach difficult spots.	

HOG RING PLIERS

Osborne No. 773-HRP

Hardened and tempered. Forged steel. Vinyl handles. Works with our new 773-K millimeters hog rings. Ideal for closing around a smaller area. Used on bungie cord.

HOG RINGS

Osborne No. 1442

Low carbon steel, bright finished. 14 Gauge. Available with sharp points or blunt points, packed in 5 or 25 lbs. Also available in stainless steel.

Osborne No. 773-K

Available in 5/8" with blunt and sharp points, and 7/8" with sharp points only. Packed in boxes of 1,000 pcs.

DIAGONAL CUTTING NIPPERS

Osborne No. 91

These rugged drop-forged nippers are ideal for cutting hog rings and wires. Polished head, black handles. 6-7/8" long.

PINCERS- FlushCut

Osborne No. 93

For heavy ripping. Polished flush cut jaws for getting close to flat surface. Overall 8". Weighs 13 oz.

SIDE CUTTERS
Side View

Osborne No. 787 A

Forged steel with extra long, pointed cutter. Polished head with vinyl handles. Depth of head aids in removing staples. This is the famous European " vienner".

WEBBING OR CANVAS PLIERS

Osborne No. 250

Made with hammer jaw; the hammer acts as a lever if a strong pull is required. An excellent tool for stretching leather and canvas. Also used as a hammer. 8-3/4" long. 3-1/2" with of jaw.

DUCK BILL PLIERS

Osborne No. 98

Jaws are hardened and tempered and carefully polished. Ideal for stretching material in tight places where space is too limited for using the ordinary stretching pliers.

ALL PURPOSE AWL

Osborne No. 18

A varied-purpose tool. It assists in the installation of roof windows, windshield rubber and back glass. Removes body clips, mouldings and for spring pulling and cotter pin extracting or for radiator hose removal. Removes staples in grooves.Great for hard to reach places.

Chapter 20 | Glossary of Tools

Safety should always be the first priority when working with any tool. Always use extreme caution and remember to wear eye protection.

Air Compressor: If you decide to use a pneumatic staple gun, you will need an air compressor. You will also need an air hose and all the fittings. I recommend quick disconnect fittings and a 1/4″ air hose. The hose should be at least 25 feet long. Some air compressors are sold with accessory kits that include the hose and all the fittings. *Tip!* Most kits include a blower gun. This is a great tool to blow the chalk residue off of fabric. A small pancake style air compressor will work fine for the do-it-yourselfer. Most air compressors will make a lot of noise while running. If the noise from an air compressor is not an issue, I would select a pneumatic stapling system.

Bronze Magnetic Tack Hammer: Has a small magnetic end on the smaller side of the head which is used for holding a tack in place. Upholstery tacks can be very small and almost impossible to hold with your fingers when hammering. Simply place tacks off to the side of your work surface and touch the small magnetic end of the hammer to the head of the tack. The tack should stay on the end of the hammer. *Tip!* Some upholsterers place the sterile tacks in their mouths and then touch the small magnetic end of the hammer to their lips. This transfers a tack to the end of the hammer and holds it in place until needed. This is where the term "spitting tacks" comes from. This small magnetic end should be used to set the tack in place. The large end of the hammer is used for hammering the tack down into the frame. I do not recommend spitting tacks for the beginner.

Button Machine: A professional tool used to make buttons. This tool and all of the accessories can be unaffordable to most do-it-yourselfers. Most local upholstery shops will make buttons for you at a minimal cost.

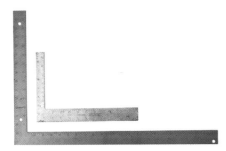

Carpenter Squares: Used to square the edges of fabrics, foams, and fillings. *Tip!* Place one side of the square along one side of the selvage edge of the fabric. Strike a chalk line on each side of the square and extend the lines from selvage to selvage and upwards along the selvage edge. This now creates a square edge to begin marking and cutting your fabric.

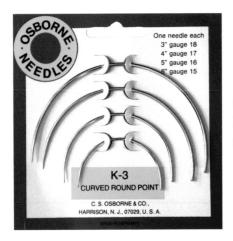

Curved Round Point Needles: Used to hand sew, a technique more commonly known as blind stitching. This eliminates the need for tacking or stapling. These needles can also be used to hand sew coil springs to webbing.

Diagonal Cutting Pliers: Helps to finish removing a staple once it has been lifted up with the staple knocker. Grasp the staple and rotate the pliers along the frame using the scooped side. *Tip!* Do not pull the staples out with the pliers. The pliers are designed to grasp and roll the staple out of the wood frame. Permanent damage can be caused to your wrists and hands by pulling out the staples.

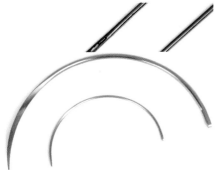

Diamond Shaped Straight and Curved Needles: Used for hand sewing vinyl, leather, filling and padding.

Fancy Nail Hammer: Similar to the tack hammer, but this hammer features a nylon tip, which is used to apply decorative nail heads. The nylon tip helps prevent damaging the ornamental nail heads.

#306 ½ Flat Regulator: Used to move irregularities or lumps underneath the final cover. It also aids in the folding of pleats, stuffing corners, pulling up welted corners, and can assist in marking cut lines. Be cautious not to puncture a hole with the regulator when working with extremely fine fabrics. Do not use a regulator to move irregularities when working with vinyl or leather.

Foam Saw / Electric Knife: Both contain two blades that move up and down and can be used to cut and shape foam padding. Keep the blades perpendicular to the foam to ensure a square cut edge.

Hog Ring Pliers: Used to install hog rings. Commonly used to install edge roll to edge wire. Also commonly used in automotive upholstering.

Klintch-It Tool: Used to install klintch-it clips that are used to fasten coil springs to jute and polypropylene webbing. This eliminates the need to hand sew the springs to the webbing.

Metal Webbing Stretcher: Used for stretching various types of metal webbing and No-Sag springs.

Safety Glasses: Eye protection worn when working with tools. These glasses should be worn especially when removing and installing staples and tacks.

Scissors/Shears: Used to cut fillings, padding, and fabrics. *Tip!* Use a smaller pair of scissors to cut fabric when trimming and at the machine sewing. Use a larger pair of scissors when cutting out the fabric at the cutting table. *Tip!* An easy to use and inexpensive cutting tool is the Black and Decker 3.6 V cordless power scissors. Cutting many pieces of fabric or several pieces of welt cord can be done in a matter of minutes and without straining your hands.

Seam Rippers: Used to remove sewn seams. They have a very sharp and pointed end that aids in cutting and removing the existing threads.

Sewing Machines: Used to sew fabrics together. Basic home sewing machines work well for the do-it-yourselfer. These machines can sew most upholstery weight fabrics. #16 needles are used for medium weight fabrics. #18 needles are used for heavy weight fabrics. Diamond pointed needles are used to sew vinyl and leather. The most commonly used foot for the sewing machine when upholstering is a welt foot. The welt foot is a specially designed foot with a groove on the bottom to help the cord stay firmly in place while being sewn into the fabric. You can purchase a welt foot for most home sewing machines. The most common size of welt cord is 5/32″. If you cannot find a welt foot for your sewing machine, use a zipper foot in its place. You can sew welt cord with a zipper foot also and by moving the needle position you can make the stitches closer to the cord.

Spring Clip Pliers: Used for applying edge wire clips to edge wire and springs.

Staple Gun: Can be manual, electric, or pneumatic. Pneumatic means air driven. When working with a staple gun, hold the head firmly against the working surface. If the head of the staple gun is tilted, the staples will not seat properly in the wood. Keep the head of the gun parallel to the edge of the wood surface apposed to perpendicular. This will achieve the maximum holding strength of the staple into the fabric. A good quality staple gun could be your largest investment. I do not recommend a manual staple gun. Not many of us have the strength or patience to use this type of staple gun. A basic electric staple gun is an inexpensive option, but you may end up hammering in the staples that did not drive all the way into a hardwood frame. I like pneumatic staple guns the best. They are lightweight, very powerful, and reasonably priced. I believe the extra long nose provides more accessibility into tight and awkward areas. I feel it is worth the few extra dollars for a long-nosed version staple gun. This same staple gun can be purchased with a shorter nose and for less money. Some shorter-nosed staple guns are less expensive and also work very well. *Tip!* Many of my students ask for hand tools, staple guns, and air compressors for their birthday, or as a Christmas gift.

Staple Knocker: Also called a staple puller or staple lifter, this tool is used to lift up staples. Diagonal cutting pliers are then used to completely remove the staple. Place one tip of the staple knocker under the staple and push firmly down on the handle. This will lift the staple up and prepare it to be removed with the diagonal cutting pliers. The side of your tack hammer or a mallet can be used to tap the end of the knocker as opposed to pushing it by hand.

Steamer: Used to remove wrinkles from fabric. Can replace the need for an iron. A steamer can also be used to soften fabrics such as vinyl. This aids in stretching the stiff fabric before stapling. *Tip!* Do not use a steamer when working with velvet and silk fabrics. The steam may cause marking or staining to these fabrics. Always test a scrap piece of fabric before using a steamer.

Straight Double Round Pointed Needles: Allows hand sewing back and forth without turning the needle.

Straight Single Round Point Needles: Are commonly used to apply buttons. They can also be used to sew heavy fillings and padding. The lengths can range from 6″ to 18″ long.

Tape Measure: Used to take measurements and works best when used on curved or rounded areas.

Upholstering Pins: Used to hold fabrics together before hand or machine sewing, tacking, or stapling.

Webbing Stretcher: Used to apply jute and polypropylene webbing.

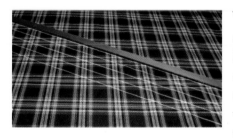

Welt Stick: Used as a guide for striking lines when making welt cords. Welt Sticks should be 1-1/2″ wide and a minimum 60″ long. *Tip!* Always cut welt cords on a bias when working with any cloth fabric. This means cutting the fabric on a diagonal. Place the welt stick on a bias and mark on each side of the stick. Share one of the existing lines and strike another line and continue until the correct number of welt cord pieces are cut. The reason the strips of welt cords are cut 1-1/2″ wide is to ensure a 1/2″ seam allowance when the cord is sewn into the strips of fabric.

Yardstick: Used to take measurements and works best on flat surfaces.

Chapter 21 | Glossary of Supplies

 **Bobbins:** Used as a bottom thread in sewing machines. Some bobbins are sold pre-wound for convenience.

  **Brass Ventilators:** Commonly used with vinyl or leather cushions to let air escape when sat upon. They are 3/4″ or 1″ in diameter and add an attractive look to the cushion when installed.

 **Burlap:** An interwoven cloth made of jute yarns or synthetic fibers. It is applied over springs and webbing in seats, arms, and back areas.

 **Button Twine:** A very strong twine normally made of nylon used to hold buttons in place. It is also used to hand sew fillings and edge roll.

 **Buttons:** Are used to hold padding firmly in place and to add a decorative look. Buttons come in several sizes. #22 is the smallest size and #60 is the largest size. The most common button has an eyelet style back. Nylon button twine is used to secure this style of button. The back of the button can also be made with a prong style back that is easily spread to keep the button in place.

Cambric: A dustproof, cotton-blended fabric used to cover the underside of furniture to achieve a finished look.

Cardboard Tack Strip: Used to attach fabric in a straight line. It gives a finished look and can be used on front boxing, outside arms, and outside backs.

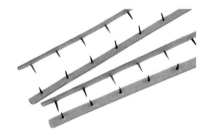

Cardboard Tack Strip with Tacks: Used on outside backs to achieve a finished edge and eliminates hand sewing. These strips are most commonly used in a vertical position and on an outside back.

Chalk: Used for marking fabrics. It comes in stick form and can be soft or hard. Soft chalk is the easiest to dust off when needed. Tailor's chalk is square and flat. Although it comes in many colors, it can leave a permanent mark.

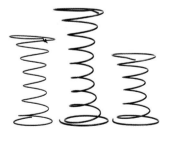

Coil Springs: Used in seats and backs. They are attached over webbing and used for support. Coil springs are available in #9 gauge metal for seats and #10 gauge metal for backs.

Cotton Batting: One of the most commonly used products for padding upholstered surfaces. Some cotton batting contains seeds and will be mixed with synthetics. These less expensive grades of cotton should be used in areas where less wear will occur. When cotton batting is used in seats, arms and backs, a higher grade of cotton should be used. *Tip!* Always tear cotton batting by hand to prevent quickly dulling your scissors or shears.

Decking: Also known as denim. This is a strong twilled usually cotton fabric, used to cover the padded deck area that is under a loose cushion. It can also be used to line the back of skirt panels.

Deck Pad: Used in the seat areas over the burlap and springs to add padding and comfort. It is a very durable synthetic material used to replace old style coconut fiber pad. *Tip!* Cotton batting can be used over the deck pad to achieve a better foundation.

Decorative Nail Heads: Used as a trim. They are commonly used over gimp trim and can be spaced or studded. Decorative nail heads come in several styles and sizes.

Double Welt Cord: Used as a decorative trim to cover the raw edges of fabric. It is most commonly used where the raw edge of the fabric meets the exposed wood.

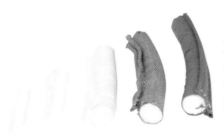

Edge Roll: Also known as jet edge, is used to pad sharp wood or spring edges. It is most commonly used on the front edges of the deck area and the front edges of the arms. It can be tacked, stapled, hand sewn, or hog ringed into place. Edge roll is made in different diameters ranging from 1/2″ to 1 1/2″.

Edge Wire: Used on the edges of coil and No-Sag springs to provide a uniformed edge and stability to the edges of the springs. It is installed after the springs have been tied and is most commonly used with loose cushion construction.

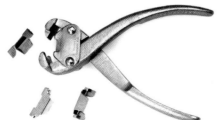

Edge Wire Clips: Used to attach the edge wire to the springs and eliminates the need to hand sew the edge wire to the springs.

Finish Nails: Used to attach front arm panels. They are very thin and have a tiny head. The nail is hammered through the fabric covered arm panel to secure the panel to the chair frame. Only arm panels covered with an open weave fabric can be installed with finish nails. If the weave of the fabric is too fine, or you are working with vinyl or leather, panel nails must be used in place of finish nails.

Foam: Made from urethane and used as padding and a cushioning base. Foam is made in several densities. Firm foams are used for seats and arms because they hold their shape. Softer, less dense foams are used for backs. Softer foams have more give and will provide more comfort but less support than the firmer and denser foams. The most common thickness of foam used for furniture cushions is 4″. The most common thickness of foam used for slip style dining room seats is 1″ to 1-1/2″. The most common thickness for capped style dining room seats is 2″. The density of foam is the weight of the foam per cubic foot. A cubic foot is 12″ × 12″ × 12″. The higher the urethane content, the denser the foam will be. A very dense foam will weigh more than a foam with a lesser urethane content. A good density for backs is 1 pound per cubic foot. A good quality for seats is 1.8–2.8 pounds per cubic foot.

The firmness or compression of urethane foam is named IFD (Indentation and Force Deflection). The designations of firmness will vary from 10 being very soft to over 100 being very firm. The most common IFD used for seating will range from 35–45.

When foam is graded you will see numbers such as 1010, 1835, or 2835. The first two numbers is the density and second two numbers is the IFD or compression rating.

The code CFR means the foam meets the California Fire Retardant specifications or CAL 117 spec. This is the industry standard.

Some foams such as closed cell foams are used for outdoor and marine applications because they are mold and mildew resistant.

Foam is cut with an electric foam saw containing two fine tooth blades positioned vertically and a flat foot on the bottom to keep the blade perpendicular to the foam. A professional foam saw can be cost prohibitive for the do-it-yourselfer. An electric carving knife can be used in place of a foam saw. Be sure to hold the knife perpendicular to the foam when cutting.

Gimp: A decorative trim used to cover the raw edge of fabric. It is most commonly used where the exposed wood edge and the raw edge of the fabric meet. Gimp is commonly applied with hot glue. Decorative nail heads can be applied over gimp trim.

Glides: Used on the bottom of legs to protect both the wood leg and the floor surface. They can be metal, nylon, or felt.

Hand Sewing Thread: Made of nylon and comes in a wide array of colors to match almost any fabric. A curved needle will commonly be used when hand sewing.

Hog Rings: Used to apply edge rolls to edge wire and springs. It also eliminates the need to hand sew the wire to the springs. Automotive upholstering is fastened to metal frames with these clips.

Hot Glue: Used to apply trims such as double welt, gimp, and fringes. Most hot glue dries clear and very quickly.

Muslin: A closely woven fabric that is used over padded areas to help shape and hold the padding in place. Muslin is rarely used in upholstering today. I feel it is an unnecessary step.

No-Sag Springs: A continuous spring used in seats and backs in place of coil springs. Heavy #9 gauge metal is used for seats and a lighter #11 gauge metal springs is used for backs. This style of spring is fastened to the frame with No-Sag clips.

Padding: Used to mold, shape, and soften furniture. The most commonly used types of padding are urethane foam, cotton, polyester, and Dacron. In years past, horse hair, straw, coconut fibers, moss, and tow were commonly used as padding. If your project is in reasonably good shape and the fillings are still intact, save them and add a fresh layer of cotton or polyester batting over the existing padding. When starting with new construction, use foam and cotton, or foam and polyester batting to create a solid foundation. Dacron is used over loose foam cushions.

Panel Nails: Used to attach pre-upholstered arm panels to the front of the arms. Panel nails are used when a finish nail cannot be used to install panels. A panel nail is hammered through the arm panel, padded over, covered with fabric and then hammered into place on the front of the arm. Panel nails work well with fine fabrics, vinyl, and leather.

Pli-Grip: A continuous metal strip used for fastening fabric on curved or straight areas. This eliminates the need for hand sewing. Pli-Grip is most commonly used on curved arms, outside wings, and arched backs.

Polyester Batting: Used as padding. It is most commonly used over foam or outside arms and outside backs of furniture to achieve a softer look and feel. Polyester batting can be cut to shape and spray glued or stapled into place. This type of batting is easier to apply than cotton because it can be glued or stapled.

Skirt Stiffener: Used in kick pleat style skirts. With the addition of this stiffener, the skirt panels remain rigid and crisp looking. The stiffener is generally made in widths ranging from 6″ to 24″.

Spray Adhesive: Commonly known as spray glue. This glue is fast tacking and very strong. It is used for bonding foam, fabric, and padding.

Spring Twine: Used to tie springs. This twine is made of polyester or natural hemp fibers. I believe the hemp twine holds a knot much better than the polyester twine. I also feel that over time the polyester twine stretches more than the natural hemp twine.

Staples: Used to hold fabric and fillings in place. Common sizes are 1/4″, 3/8″, and 9/16″. Stainless steel staples are recommended for marine or outdoor use because they will not rust.

Stronghold Nails: Also known as ring shank nails, they are threaded and used for maximum withdrawal resistance. They are commonly used to hold no-sag spring clips and steel webbing in place.

Tee-Nuts: A fastening system used to hold dining room chair seats and arms to the chair frame. A machine thread screw is used with the tee-nut.

Thread: #69 nylon is the most commonly used thread by the professional upholsterer because it is very strong. Most home sewing machines will not be able to sew with this thread. Polyester, or a blend of cotton and polyester, is a good choice for most home sewing machines.

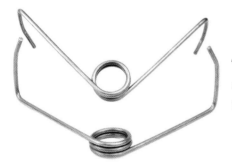

Torsion Springs: These springs add extra strength and support to the front coil and No-Sag springs. They are secured to the edge wire with edge wire clips and the other end is fastened to the frame with No Sag clips.

Upholstery Tacks: Packaged in sterile boxes and come in a wide array of sizes. The sizes have numbers associated with them. The smaller the number, the smaller the tack. The numbers range from #2 to #14. The #4 tacks and the #6 tacks are often used to tack fabric and fillings in place. The #12 tacks and the #14 tacks are commonly used to apply webbing to the seat areas.

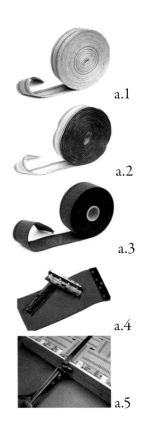

a.1

a.2

a.3

a.4

a.5

Webbing: Used as a foundation for seats, backs, and arms. Coil springs, foam, and padding is installed on top of the webbing. Webbing is 3-1/2″ wide and is made of jute (Figure a.1) or polypropylene (Figure a.2). Elastic webbing is 2″ to 3″ in width. Elastic webbing flexes for comfort and eliminates the use of the springs in seats and backs (Figure a.3). Rubber webbing is 2″ wide and is used in Danish modern style furniture. It also flexes but cushions are commonly placed directly on top of the rubber webbing. Rubber webbing can be installed with specially designed clips or it can be stapled or tacked into place (Figure a.4). Rubber and elastic webbing can be installed with a rubber & elastic webbing stretcher. Steel webbing is approximately 1″ wide and can be solid or perforated. Steel webbing is used to help support jute or polypropylene webbing. It is stretched over each strip of webbing, interwoven and secured to the frame with stronghold or ring shank nails. A specialty tool called a metal webbing stretcher must be used to apply this type of webbing (Figure a.5).

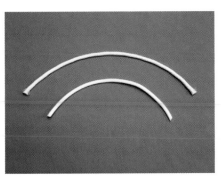

Welt Cord: A strong, round, rope-like material used in the making of piping or welt cord. Welt cord is made from paper, cellulose, jute, or polyethylene. The most common size of welt cord is 5/32″. Once covered with fabric, welt cord is used as a decorative trim on the edges of a frame, above skirts, and in the seams on cushions and pillows. The polyethylene welt cord is used for outdoor and marine use because it will not rot.

Wood Dowel Pins: Used to join furniture frames together. The grooves in the dowels help to spread the glue throughout the joint. They are made in various lengths and diameters.

Wood Glue: Used in the construction and repairs of wood frames. Water resistant glues should be used when working with marine and outdoor projects.

Wood Plugs: Used to cover the heads of countersunk wood screws. The plugs are made in a wide variety of shapes and sizes. They can be stained to match the furniture's wood color.

Zippers: Used in pillows and cushions to close two pieces of fabric together. Zippers are made of nylon, brass, or aluminum. Zippers have numbers associated with them to indicate the size of the tooth on the zipper. The larger the number, the larger the tooth. The #5 zipper is the most commonly used zipper in upholstering because it is very durable. Nylon zippers are used in marine or outdoor applications because they will not rot.

Chapter 22 | Glossary of Terminology

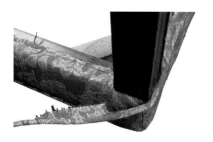

Base Welt: A decorative, fabric-covered, rope-like trim added to the bottom of furniture, such as dining room chair seats. The welt trim is cut on the bias in 1-1/2″ strips. A rope like material is sewn in the center of the strip and then it is stapled into place.

Basting Stitch: A temporary long stitch made on the sewing machine that can be easily removed. This stitch is commonly used when sewing a zipper track.

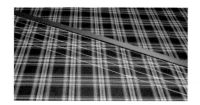

Bias: To cut on a slant or diagonal. Fabric used to make welt cord should be cut on the bias. This adds strength and wearability to the fabric and also makes it easier to tailor.

Blind Stitch: A stitch made when hand sewing two pieces of fabric together. A curved needle is commonly used when sewing a blind stitch. *Tip!* The key to hand-sewing a blind stitch is to keep the stitches parallel to each other. This prevents the fabric from bunching.

Blind Tack: A technique used to replace blind stitching or any hand sewing. Cardboard tack strip is stapled over the backside of the fabric and the fabric is then pulled and stapled into place. This technique is commonly used on the top of outside arms and the top of outside backs.

Boxed Edge: The term used to describe the edge of a cushion. This edge is sewn with boxing between the two faces. A welt cord or other type of trim may be added to the boxing.

Boxing: The strip of fabric between the top and bottom of the cushion faces.

Crowned: To add loft or height to a cushion or pillow. An outward bow should be cut into the fabric if the cushion or pillow is to have a large amount of loft. This bow will keep the edge of the cushion straight when filled with a lofted filling.

Double Welt: Used as a decorative trim, it is most commonly used to cover the raw edge of fabric where it meets a decorative wood surface. This welt trim is cut on the bias and in 2-1/2″ to 3″ strips. To make this welt trim, fold over only 1-1/2″ of the fabric and sew a welt cord into place using a welt foot on the sewing machine. After the first cord is sewn into place, a second cord will be sewn. Place the second cord (tightly) next to the first sewn cord and roll the entire piece over. Sew the two cords together by sewing down the center of the two cords and on the previous sew line. Work with about six to eight inches at one time. Finally, trim the remaining tail off of the backside of the trim and hot glue the trim to the desired area.

Drop Match: Drop-matched patterns do not have the same pattern from side to side on the 54″ width of fabric, they are staggered. (In most cases, if you split the 54″ width of fabric, the patterns on the fabric will look the same on each side. This enables you to split the width of fabric and cut two of the same items such as both arm pieces and cushion tops out of the 54″ width of fabric.) When using a drop-matched pattern, the cushion top is cut from one side of the fabric, then you will need to drop down (unroll) the other side of the fabric to find the same pattern to match. Drop-matched patterns normally require more fabric for matching when upholstering and are better suited for drapery making.

Face: The correct side of the fabric.

Hand Sew: A technique used to join two or more items together. A curved needle and a blind stitch is commonly used when hand sewing.

Knife Edge: To have only one seam on an edge of a pillow or cushion. A welt cord or other type of trim may be added to the seam.

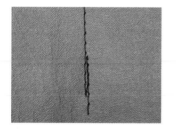

Lockstitch: Added stitches to secure, lock, or add strength to the seamed area. When using a sewing machine, a reverse stitch is commonly used.

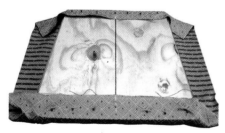

Loose Tack: A temporary means of holding fabric in place until stapled. The tack is hammered only part of the way into place making it easy to remove when needed.

Mirror Image: To show the opposite image as if you were looking into a mirror. Arms, wings, and arm panels should be applied to show the mirror image of each other to achieve a professional look.

Mitered: To join together with an angle. Most corners on the deck area are made with a mitered cut.

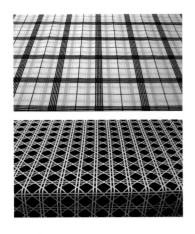

Non-Directional: Patterned fabric that can be cut "up the roll" or "railroaded", either direction is proper. Once decided upon, continue cutting all the pieces in the same direction.

Railroaded: The patterns or stripes are woven or printed from selvage to selvage, as opposed to "up the roll". This allows you to cut endless lengths of fabric without having to seam the patterns together. When working with long cushions or items such as sofas that are longer than 54", there is no need to sew widths of fabric together to achieve the desired lengths. This generally saves fabric and a great deal of time.

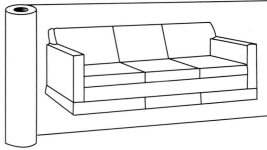

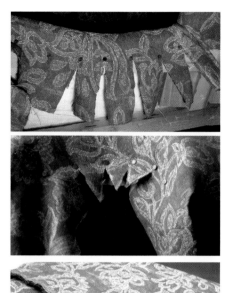

Relief Cuts: Small cuts made generally on curved areas to help the fabric conform to the desired shape.

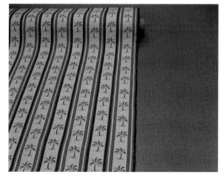

Seam Allowance: The amount of extra fabric added to an item to be sewn. The most common seam allowance in upholstering is 1/2″.

Selvage: A woven edge that prevents fabric from unraveling. The selvages are located on each edge of the fabric and should be removed before cutting the fabric pieces.

Slip Seat: A style of dining room seat. The fabric is wrapped around a padded wooden board, secured with staples or tacks and sewing is not involved. The seats are commonly attached to the chair with screws. A base welt trim can be added for a more decorative appearance.

Tight Seat: A style of seat where the fabric is pulled around the padded area and permanently secured to the frame with staples or tacks. A loose cushion will not be applied over this area.

Top Stitch: An added stitch to a seam to enhance the appearance and or strength of the seam. This decorative stitch can be on one or both sides of the seam.

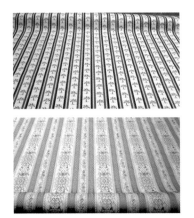

Up The Roll: The patterns or stripes are woven or printed "up the roll" of fabric similar to wallpaper as opposed to being woven or printed from selvage to selvage.

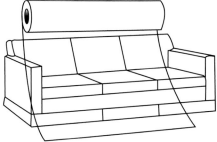

Welt Cord: A decorative, fabric-covered rope-like trim used in seams and on the edges of furniture. If the welt cord is being made of the same fabric it is called self-welt. If the welt is being made in a different fabric it is called contrasting-welt.

Special Thanks

Technical Advice / Graphic Design & Layout
Matt Walters
Wudyaget Field Portraits
www.wudyaget.com
sales@wudyaget.com

Gina Destro

Legal Advice
Stephen R. Cook, Esq.
The University of Akron
Clinical Professor of Law
Director, New Business Legal Clinic
scook@uakron.edu

Shannon Foreman
Law Student
The University of Akron School of Law
Sjf20@uakron.edu

Photography
Glossary of Tools, Glossary of Supplies, Touching Up the Wood
Photography provided by
Nathan P. Destro
NPD Photography
www.npdphotography.com
destrovision@gmail.com

Conclusion

Iam very glad I listened to my students, family, and friends. Their overwhelming encouragement and support led me to write this book.

I enjoyed writing this book and look forward to writing my next. The next book will be more advanced. Some of the techniques I would like to discuss in my next book are button tufting, channel backs, and sewing different styles of cushions. Yes, again you will receive *All the Trade Secrets.*

Let me know your thoughts and feelings regarding this book. How can I make my next book better? Was the book easy to follow? Did you find all of the *Tips!* helpful? Was the book illustrated to your satisfaction? Let me know what you would like to see in my next book.

Feel free to visit my web site www.ClevelandUpholstering.com to view samples of my work, ask me questions and please, send me pictures of all your projects! They just may be included in my next book!

You may contact me via e-mail or write to me at the following address.

Web Site ----- www.GrindstonePublishing.com

E-mail ------ Frank@GrindstonePublishing.com

Address ---- Grindstone Publishing, LLC
                Frank T. Destro, Jr.
                7109 Timber Lane
                Olmsted Falls, Ohio USA 44138-1175

Thank You,

Frank T. Destro, Jr.

Index

Page numbers in **bold** indicate glossary references.

About the Author

Frank T. Destro, Jr. is a successful upholsterer, instructor, and a true craftsman with over 30 years of experience. He is highly regarded by his students, clients, business associates, and peers. Twice he has been featured in Cleveland's, *The Plain Dealer*, including a Cover Story and a CareerScape article. He was quoted in *Marine Textiles Magazine*, and a guest speaker at the *Westlake Ohio Department of Community Services*. He has instructed hundreds of students in his one-of-a-kind, Professional Upholstering classes.

Many students have encouraged Frank to share his unique teaching style with others by writing a book. This led to the creation of this complete, educational, and easy to follow how-to guide for the do-it-yourselfer as well as the skilled craftsman. Frank knows he can show anyone how simple Professional Upholstering can be, if you know ...

All the Trade Secrets.

Notes